FROM THE HANDS
OF HEROES

The St Paul's Cathedral First World War
Altar Frontal and Memorial Book

ISBN 978-0-9955418-0-1

Printed and bound in Poland

CONTENTS

The St Paul's Cathedral First World War Altar Frontal: An Appreciation

by The Reverend Canon Michael Hampel

It is with such faith and such hope that we pray for the time when God will beat people's swords into ploughshares and their spears into pruning hooks. But, as conflict continues in the many troubled parts of our world, it seems but an ideal dream more than any near-present reality.

The story of humankind is the story of one bloody mess after another so that the Christmas carol is horribly accurate when it says that man at war with man hears not the love song which the angels bring.

In July 1919, the nation gathered in St Paul's Cathedral to give thanks that one war at least was over. The newspaper reports of the time recall a sombre mood: an exhausted and troubled people were in no mood to celebrate.

'The Daily Telegraph' described the scene: 'Grave and subdued was the whole setting in the soft light of a morning overcast with clouds; yet to those who sat under the dome facing towards the sacrarium there was the beautiful radiance of the altar, embodying a symbolism of poignant and splendid appeal. The new altar frontal ... is the offering and work of soldiers so disabled that they can only undertake tasks involving no physical exertion. The richest white satin forms the ground. In the centre panel is the chalice, suggested, it is said, by a lad of 19, as the fitting emblem of sacrifice, and surely implying a noble submission to suffering in the words "the cup which My Father hath sent shall I not drink it?" ... On either side are crossed palms embroidered in gold by men who kept the flag flying at sea to their own grievous wounding; while the bordering includes the rose, alike of mystical and national significance, wrought with conventional foliage in artistic colourings.'

Only eight days before this special service attended by the King and Queen, the Treaty of Versailles had been signed, containing terms and conditions which, many would say, sowed the seeds for the rise of Nazism and a Second World War only twenty years later – a war which saw St Paul's Cathedral directly hit several times, the altar for which this frontal was made destroyed, and the work of our soldier embroiderers consigned to a storage chest for the next 74 years.

Anniversaries of war are no occasions for celebration and, if anything, provide moments of recognition that all is not well with the world. And yet people of faith are obliged to express hope despite everything – and the altar frontal, the subject of this book, articulates – both physically and aesthetically – a legacy: lest we forget.

The altar frontal is itself a legacy in textile and great artistry – and one which occupied the work and attention of staff and volunteers at the Cathedral for many months, for which we are deeply grateful: because this legacy has itself acted as a catalyst for our remembrance which is its own legacy because memory is the mind's eye which – firmly fixed on the past – informs our actions now and in the future. But there is another legacy which has been drawn to St Paul's since the altar frontal project began – and this is the relatives of the men who made this beautiful cloth.

Some of them remembered their forebears talking about the St Paul's altar frontal; to others, news that they were related to someone who had made an altar frontal for St Paul's Cathedral came as a complete surprise – but, either way, they travelled to St Paul's from Australia, Canada and around the United Kingdom, drawn by something good and beautiful and used in the service of Christ's Church, to remember and to give thanks for the British, Australian, Canadian, New Zealand and South African men who expressed hope despite everything and whose swords were turned by that very hope not into ploughshares but into embroidery needles.

One of the most heartening things we learnt during the project is just how many of our soldier artists carried on their embroidery for the rest of their lives. How I love the story of Driver Percy Cooney of the Royal Field Artillery who was stitching regimental badges when Queen Alexandra visited him in the Royal National Orthopaedic Hospital in London and asked for one of his badges but he refused, telling Her Majesty that it was for his sister, Mabel. On recounting the story many years later, his wife was horrified to learn that her husband had turned down a request from the Queen! But he found another piece of embroidery for his royal visitor and she subsequently sent him a crested tin with cigarettes and cigars and a five pound note. She was also present at the memorial service at St Paul's in 1919 with her son, George V, and her daughter-in-law, Queen Mary – gazing as our visitors do at the work of Driver Cooney and his comrades. Perhaps he was here too, the cigarette tin carefully stowed away in his pocket ready to light up once he got back out onto Ludgate Hill later that morning.

I believe keenly that the creative spirit is in every human being by very virtue of the fact that we are human creatures of the divine creator. If we read the creation story imaginatively, it becomes clear that to be made in the image of God means that we are most God-like when we are being creative which suggests that we are most devilish when we are being destructive.

The story of this altar frontal demonstrates how our creative spirit can be harnessed as a means of rehabilitation – palliative and restorative, redemptive even. But I wonder if we, a hundred years on, need to work harder to harness the creative spirit not just to restore but to prevent.

It is an old adage that prevention is better than cure. One great example of the creative spirit being harnessed to prevent hatred and to break down barriers is Daniel Barenboim's West Eastern Divan Orchestra in which Arabs and Israelis make music together in harmony and in peace. It is hard to imagine that the hands that lift a violin to the shoulder and slide a bow across the strings to produce a sound of great beauty could also lift a gun to the shoulder and pull a trigger.

Might another legacy of this altar frontal be a greater commitment on the part of all of us, and of the world beyond the walls of St Paul's Cathedral, to place into more people's hands the tools of artistry and creativity so that people are so occupied in building up that they have no time to take up arms; are so occupied in building bridges that they have no enemies against whom to take aim and fire; are so occupied in building hope that they will carry on doing so despite everything.

It may sound naive but, God help us, it works: the Ashington miners weren't good with words so they painted; the unemployed of the Great Depression opened theatres as part of the Settlement movement; Fine Cell Work is a social enterprise that trains prisoners in paid, skilled, creative needlework to foster hope, discipline and self-esteem; Michael Bogdanov moved into the inner city estate of Ladywood in Birmingham and turned indifference, suspicion and hostility into an eighty-strong cast to stage extracts from Shakespeare; and Gareth Malone has reminded people that they can sing despite what they were told when they were kids.

Nearly 150 men learned to embroider despite experiencing horrors that we hardly dare to imagine. To the greater glory of God and in their memory, I would like us all to call the world's attention to the creative spirit that God has implanted in his children and to work actively – not only reactively – to the potential of human creativity to beat swords into ploughshares and spears into pruning hooks so that we be worthy of the name 'children of God' because we are peacemakers and are blessed for that.

This altar frontal is the golden thread that weaves together our remembrance with our aspirations. Like our faith, it expresses hope despite everything and it is a legacy that not only pleads for peace but provides us with a method for peace.

This is based on the sermon given by the Reverend Canon Michael Hampel on the eve of the hundredth anniversary of the outbreak of World War One at St Paul's Cathedral, when the altar frontal was used at a celebration of the Eucharist at which the Bishop of London, the Right Reverend Richard Chartres, presided.

Michael Hampel
St Paul's Cathedral

FROM THE HANDS
OF HEROES

AN INTRODUCTION

No cathedral in Britain better embodies the Christian concepts of resurrection, rebirth and renewal than St Paul's, Sir Christopher Wren's defining masterpiece. The cathedral emerged from the ashes after its predecessor, started by the Normans in 1087 and completed in 1240, was burned down in the Great Fire of London in 1666. According to the legend established in 'Parentalia', the Wren family memoir, the great architect surveyed the empty site and instructed a common labourer to bring him a flat stone from a heap of rubble with which he could mark the centre of what would be the new cathedral. The labourer returned with a broken stone - part of a gravestone, it seemed - on which a single word could be seen: 'Resurgam', Latin for 'I shall rise again'.

It was appropriate, then, that Wren's masterpiece should be the channel through which a group of wounded servicemen found a kind of rebirth after the horrors of the First World War. At least 138 men from all branches of the armed forces, and from South Africa, Australia, New Zealand and Canada as well as Britain, put their skills to work on a complex and intricate piece of embroidery - a new ornamental frontal for the high altar at St Paul's. Working on the frontal gave these men an opportunity not only to recover and develop their motor skills but to find camaraderie and hope in the process of creating what, to all intents and purposes, was a brand new work of art. Such work was, as the testimony of the families of some of the servicemen suggests, not just a profound aid in the men's path back to health but a means of rediscovering beauty and meaning after witnessing such slaughter and suffering.

That the frontal was also a tribute from the men themselves to their fallen comrades was underlined by the symbolism of the design, particularly the inclusion of flowers and birds, and the frontal's intended role in Holy Communion, the ceremony given to the apostles by Christ as a vehicle for remembrance. This aspect took on a more personal nature in the Memorial Book that was compiled to accompany the frontal, in which the men involved were listed and to which the hospitals contributed their own comemmorative pages.

Viewed at a distance of a hundred years, the pages of the Memorial Book are as moving and telling as the frontal fabric itself, and more than worthy of reproduction in a volume such as this. Some are fully finished, others only half realised, while a few are barely started at all - a pointer, perhaps, to the huge and often rapid turnover in the injured who passed through the hospitals. Together they offer a valuable insight into hospital life during the First World War and the mind set of those who took their first steps to recovery and rehabilitation in the walls of these remarkable institutions. Most of all, however, the story of the frontal and its accompanying Memorial Book is a story of resilience - a triumph of personal and collective endeavour over the brutalising effects of war.

The creation of the altar frontal

Much of the precise history behind the making of the altar frontal and the Memorial Book is, sadly, lost to time. We cannot even be sure who commissioned the work, though the go ahead must have been given at the highest level within St Paul's as the frontal had to match the dimensions of the existing high altar, which had been constructed only three decades earlier in 1888.

What is certain is that the original design and much of the work in co-ordinating the project was undertaken by the Royal School of Needlework (RSN), which was founded in 1872 as the School of Art Needlework. Queen Victoria became its Patron from 1875. Under the presidency of her third daughter, Princess Helena, it grew in tandem with the Arts and Crafts Movement led by the textile designer and poet William Morris, who himself created an altar frontal for the cathedral at Bradford, a city with a long and proud textile heritage. Its 1880 publication 'Handbook of Embroidery' was a hugely influential work.

Work on the altar frontal may have started as early as July 1918 and was almost certainly completed by the signing of the Treaty of Versailles in June 1919 that brought a formal end to the war. Where dates appear in the Memorial Book, they suggest that the hospitals in question had submitted their parts of the embroidery by April 1919, in time for the pieces to be taken to the RSN's headquarters in Exhibition Road in South Kensington to be sewn together.

Unfortunately we know little about the tutors at the RSN or the many individual volunteers and medical staff in the hospitals who guided and treated the men, nor can we put an exact name to who created the beautiful altar frontal design that they

followed. We can perhaps take an informed guess at the latter: the most likely candidate is Nellie Whichelo (pictured left), an associate of William Morris and head of the workroom at the RSN, where she was responsible for a number of designs for screens and altar frontals such as that for Portsmouth Cathedral in 1907. A set of her hangings, worked by RSN stitchers, won a gold medal at the Paris Exhibition of 1900. The aunt of the novelist E. M. Forster, she worked at the RSN all her career, from 1879 to 1939, and was the School's longest serving employee. Her work was shown in the exhibitions of the Arts and Crafts Exhibition Society alongside that by Edward Burne-Jones and Walter Crane. The St Paul's altar frontal has much of the grace and understated elegance of the Whichelo style.

Thanks to the superb research undertaken by St Paul's volunteer Jane Robinson, a Friend of St Paul's Cathedral and a Conservation Patron, and St Paul's archivist Sarah Radford, we do know something of the men who embroidered the altar frontal, and some of their stories are briefly told in the pages that follow. Many service records of the Great War period were destroyed in air raids during the Second World War, but through Jane and Sarah's work we know where and with whom the men served, the circumstances of their injuries, the point at which they resumed their lives in peace time, and much more besides. Without their skill and tenacity in tracing the men from the available records and contacting many of their families, the stories would have remained unlocked and this book would have been impossible to produce.

The culture of remembrance

To trace the purpose and thinking behind the altar frontal, we need to place it in the context of the years 1916-17 and the culture of remembrance that was developing in response to the unprecedented scale of war casualties. As early as 1916, over 200 war cemeteries were commissioned in France and Belgium under the auspices of the Imperial (later Commonwealth) War Graves Commission, prompting debate about what longer term memorials might be appropriate. This would eventually lead to the construction of huge cemeteries in northern France and Belgium and the unveiling of the Cenotaph in London in 1920 as a focus of national remembrance. In villages, towns and cities across the nation, similar plans were discussed, argued over and enacted, with the result that now, a century later, there remain few places in Britain without a war memorial of some kind.

But there were also memorials of a more abstract kind, created or commissioned by individuals, organisations, schools, colleges, companies, churches and even suburban streets as a mark of respect for their war dead and a focus for those who survived. The altar frontal created for St Paul's was one such, and its role as a memorial to sacrifice was widely reported in the press at the time of its dedication on 5th July 1919 in a service led by William Inge, Dean of St Paul's. It was used during the following day's national service of thanksgiving attended by King George V and Queen Mary, when a hundred thousand people lined the streets leading to the cathedral.

As it happened, the new frontal (pictured right on the original high altar) was used only intermittently after its dedication, possibly for fear of damaging its fabric, but it was always in place for Remembrance Day each year. When the Luftwaffe began attacking London in the late summer of 1940, St Paul's was at obvious risk and the frontal was stored for safe keeping. It was therefore spared when, on the night of 10th October, the high altar was destroyed during an air raid. A new high altar was commissioned after the war and finally completed in 1958 but, because its dimensions were different from the original altar, the frontal proved unsuitable for use.

In 2013, with the centenary of the outbreak of the Great War approaching, the frontal was brought out of storage and revealed in all its beauty for the first time in decades. It then became the subject of a major restoration project undertaken by a skilled team of volunteer broderers. On 3rd August 2014, the frontal was rededicated at a service attended by relatives of some of the servicemen involved and representatives of the British Government and the High Commissions of Australia, Canada, New Zealand and South Africa. The next day the restored piece was put on display at St Paul's for the duration of the centenary commemorations. The aim of the display, as explained by the Reverend Canon Michael Hampel, the Precentor of St Paul's, was to encourage prayer and reflection during the four years of the centenary. Beside it was displayed a facsimile of the Memorial Book - the original too fragile to put on show - containing individual pages contributed by the original participating hospitals. Each page of the Memorial Book is reproduced in this publication, along with a representation of the altar frontal itself.

Handicrafts as therapy

Well before the outbreak of war in 1914, embroidery had become an accepted part of therapeutic practice for patients adjusting to disabilities alongside other handicrafts and manual skills such as metalwork and gardening. Basketwork was much encouraged among those affected by nervous conditions, to the point that 'basket case' entered the language as a disparaging term for the mentally disturbed or traumatised.

The roots of therapeutic treatment in general - and what became known as occupational therapy after the war - lay in the enlightened approaches to mental health practised during what became known as the Moral Treatment era of the early 19th century. Led by Quakers in Britain and the United States, who established their own pioneering hospitals, this was a movement based on treating people with psychiatric disorders in a humane way. One such hospital, Sheppard Asylum in Philadelphia, included on its staff the psychiatrist William Rush Dunton, who was an early proponent of the use of quilt making in rehabilitation. Another pioneer was Eleanor Clark Slagle of Johns Hopkins University in Baltimore, who went on to open the first professional school for occupational therapy.

The coming of conflict in 1914 brought huge new medical challenges as the new machinery of 20th century warfare caused injuries of a nature and on a scale never seen before. Their impact was often worsened by appalling conditions in the trenches, as most amputations were performed not as a result of the injuries themselves but because of the rapid onset of gangrene. The scars were not just physical, of course: the blanket term 'neurasthenia' was freely applied to any kind of war-related nervous disorder, but 'shell shock' was regarded much more ambivalently and was not even accepted as genuine in the highest military circles. Treatment could vary from extreme electric shock therapy to the 'talking cure' approach of Dr William Rivers at Craiglockhart Hospital in Scotland, whose patients included the officer poets Siegfried Sassoon and Wilfred Owen.

Therapeutic approaches to mental and physical recovery were actively encouraged by the military in Canada, where the Canadian Military Hospitals Commission appointed Thomas Kidner as Vocational Secretary in 1916. He introduced a regime of occupational work for men in his care. Also influential was a French physiologist named Jules Amar who developed instruments to measure the effectiveness of war injury rehabilitation. There was no uniform approach, however, and such was the pressure to get the injured back to the front - the prime aim of treatment, after all - that therapy at many military hospitals in Britain was not just unguided and improvised but highly reliant on external help.

The role of embroidery
Embroidery was a largely uncontroversial element in the therapeutic mix during the Great War. In stitching a fabric, the convalescing servicemen at the military hospitals - all dressed uniformly in their 'hospital blues' of a blue jacket, blue trousers, a white shirt and a red necktie - would find solace, inspiration and a measure of pride. The act of sewing would add focus and purpose to their recovery, while improving their hand co-ordination and allaying boredom and melancholy. As a lap craft, embroidery could be attempted while seated in a chair or upright in bed, as the photograph below shows. As the 'Yorkshire Post' reported on activities at a local military hospital in July 1917, 'the men take readily to embroidery and other artistic work suitable to their physical capacity, and the employment has not only revealed a wealth of unsuspected talent but, by keeping their minds alert and occupied, has greatly facilitated progress towards convalescence.'

Hospitals could draw on a wide number of organisations and individuals, nationally and locally, to provide teaching in needlework skills. The Red Cross Society led the way in providing tutelage in handicrafts to its own hospitals while one of the founders of the Embroiderers Guild, Bradford-born Louisa Pesel, started an embroidery section at her home city's Abram Peel Hospital, which specialised in treating neurological disorders. She helped some of her patients to embroider the Khaki Cloth, a cross-stitch frontlet made for use at services in the Abram Peel Hospital and later restored, like the St Paul's altar frontal, for the centenary of the

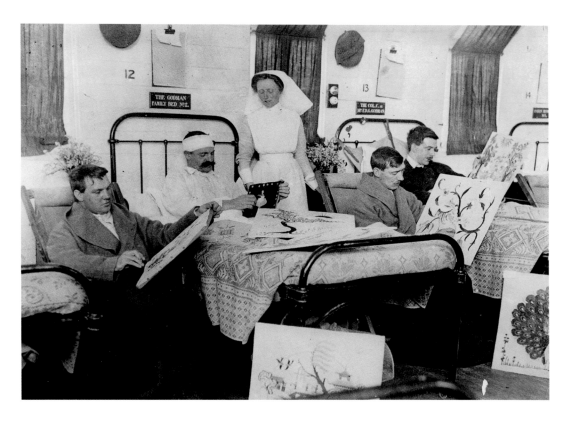

Great War. Another pioneer, though again unrecognised at the time, was the actor and professional embroiderer Ernest Thesiger, who was wounded in France and found his own way back to health through needlework. He later started a scheme for soldiers in hospital based on providing canvases for patients to work on.

Many Victorian institutions such as asylums for the mentally afflicted had used manual work such as gardening and laundry as part of their regime, with the more enlightened adopting more expressive craft-oriented therapies as time went on. When military hospitals mushroomed in Britain at the start of the war, some former asylums were converted into specialist hospitals and employed some of the same staff, whose instinct was to follow similar policies. The Welsh Metropolitan Hospital, for example, was formerly the Cardiff City Asylum. A tablecloth now on display at the National Museum of Wales was embroidered there by recovering servicemen with help from local embroidery teachers. It was signed by its Medical Superintendent, Lieutenant-Colonel Edwin Goodall, who was awarded a CBE after the war for his pioneering work with shell shocked patients.

Educationalists also played their part in promoting the benefits of needlework as therapy. A book published just before the war, 'Educational Needlecraft' by Margaret Swanson and Ann Macbeth, broke new ground by offering a complete needlework scheme for practical use in schools. Ann Macbeth herself had designed a communion table frontal for Glasgow Cathedral and, as a teacher and embroidery specialist at Glasgow School of Art, she sent her students to a hospital in Reading to work with recovering patients.

Embroidery in everyday life
It is important to note just how much a part embroidery played in the everyday life of the nation at this time. A major pastime for middle class women from early Victorian times, its popularity burgeoned after the invention of the hot iron transfer in the 1870s. Two rival companies, William Briggs of Manchester and William Deighton of London, claimed the process as their own and dominated the market by producing transfers that enabled anyone with basic ability to produce patterns or designs that were colourful and rewarding. Both produced patriotic and regimental badge transfers for sale to the public in retail stores during the Great War.

Was there any reluctance on the part of Britain's fighting men to engage in what was regarded traditionally as women's work? Certainly some eyebrows were raised that such a 'feminine' task should be encouraged in men trained to kill, but it was by no means unknown for men to pick up a needle and thread, especially when in military service. Far from being seen as an unmanly pursuit, basic sewing was one of the secondary skills that a man of the forces was expected to have, to keep his buttons secure and his uniform in trim but also - in the case of sailors - to perform vital tasks such as repairing sails. Sewing kits were an essential part of the kit of every soldier and officer during the Great War and beyond.

Soldiers were also encouraged to take up sewing as recreation, to distract them from the less salubrious pursuits of drinking and gambling. This was always going to be a losing battle, yet thousands of soldiers and sailors did make elaborate sweetheart pin-cushions to send home as tokens of their devotion. By the Great War, the pin-cushions would include pre-printed ribbons bearing messages such as 'Think of me' and possibly the serviceman's regiment or division.

Embroidery as a skill was also highly valued within the military: ornately embroidered regimental badges were a source of pride and enormous care and expense was taken over them. Military quilts - sometimes known as Crimean quilts because of their association with that conflict - were made from wool serge or woven worsted twill used in the production of military uniforms, in keeping with the Victorian fashion for colourful and elaborate patchwork.

Exhibitions, sales and local initiatives

There was a strong fund raising aspect to all this activity. Complementing the flag days held every week for charitable causes, many military hospitals encouraged their patients to create work that could be sold at periodic exhibitions or bazaars and fetes. Local competitions were often held, with winning servicemen receiving certificates or small prizes. Rarely would a week go by without local or regional newspapers reporting on an event or fund raising drive at the neighbourhood military hospital centred on the craft skills of its patients. An edition of the 'Herts and Essex Observer' in June 1918 reported that a sale of work at the VAD Hospital in Bishop's Stortford - where at least one of the contributors to the St Paul's altar frontal was treated - raised £102 for the hospital's Cigarette, Needlework and Comforts Fund.

A letter to 'The Times' in November 1916 appealing for funds for the Handicrafts Committee at the huge Netley hospital explained that 'the way in which interesting employment contributes to the recovery of the invalids has been testified to both by doctors and nurses ... many a depressed and desponding patient has taken fresh courage with the knowledge that useful and, above all, creative work is yet possible to him.' Describing the involvement of the Ladies Needlework Guild in tutoring injured servicemen, the 'Aberdeen Journal' noted in December 1917 that 'employment of this kind is welcomed by those soldiers who are unable to go out, and helps to pass many a weary hour, as well as being advantageous from a medical point of view.' That same month a reporter for the 'Dundee Courier' wrote of a display at the Recreation Hut at Dundee War Hospital that the work 'merited the high praise of an embroidery expert who remarked of some of the pieces that they would not have been done better by experienced feminine embroiderers.'

What the 'Birmingham Mail' in a May 1917 article called 'the teaching of recreative crafts in the local hospitals' was inaugurated in Birmingham thanks to the influence of the Lady Mayoress, Mrs Neville Chamberlain, and was partly financed by the Lady Mayoress's Depot, which funded and co-ordinated much of the war-related charitable work in the city. 'Scores of ladies are engaged each week in the larger hospitals in teaching the soldiers such activities as embroidery,' the article stated, '[while] some of the sick and wounded men have proved very apt and clever and have done extraordinarily good and artistic work.'

As the Lady Mayoress's involvement suggests, local charitable initiatives underpinned the drive to get military hospitals opened in their locality and patients sewing. This was a golden era for volunteers and benefactors, especially among middle and upper class women blessed with a passionate campaigning spirit and a never-take-no-for-an-answer attitude that could often be the bane of the Whitehall ministries. Several of the military hospitals whose patients worked on the St Paul's altar frontal were in fact founded by such campaigners.

Britain's military hospitals

One of the lessons of the South African wars was that the nation should have plans in place for treatment of the wounded if another war occurred. In 1909 a new 'Scheme for the Organisation of Voluntary Aid in England and Wales' was drawn up, leading the Red Cross and St John Ambulance to create separate male and female Voluntary Aid Detachments (VADs) to staff auxiliary hospitals. Military hospitals came to depend not just on a huge volunteer force of nursing staff, some from as far afield as India and Japan, but on vast charitable contributions.

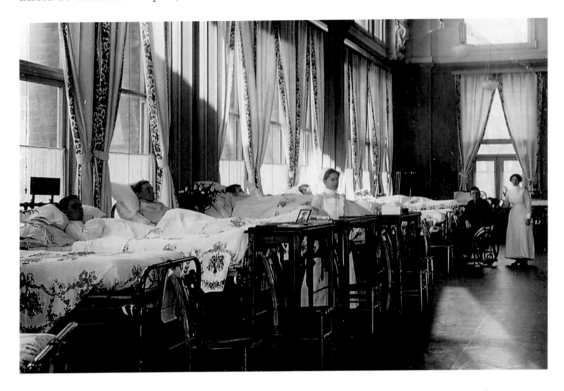

Once war was declared, many large private homes were donated for transformation into hospitals, including the most northerly of the military hospitals represented in the Memorial Book, Durris Auxiliary Red Cross Hospital in Kincardineshire. The hospital was established at Kirkton Hall and was part of the estate of the Baird family. Among the most southerly was the Lady George Nevill Hospital, founded in 1917 by the wife of the third son of the Marquess of Abergavenny. On a visit to a hospital in London, Lady George had been so moved by the number of patients affected by shell shock that she started a fund to set up a specialist hospital adjacent to her home on Palmeira Square in Hove, Sussex, which became the neurological section of the 2nd Eastern General Hospital. Her own son Captain Rupert Nevill died there on 3rd November 1918, just eight days before the Armistice.

The American banker Otto Kahn lent his London residence, St Dunstan's Lodge near Regent's Park, to a charity for blinded servicemen set up in 1915 by future 'Daily Express' founder Arthur Pearson. Having lost his own sight through glaucoma, Pearson was appalled by general indifference to blindness and created the Blinded Soldiers' and Sailors' Care Committee. St Dunstan's Lodge duly opened as a hostel with assistance from the Red Cross and a grant from the National Relief Fund. Pearson's aim was to give servicemen who had been blinded the care and rehabilitation they needed to lead constructive, self-sufficient lives. Blind soldiers and sailors were taught new skills including needlework. By the end of 1918, over 1,300 servicemen were either receiving training or had been trained there. The charity retained the name of St Dunstan's until 2012, when it became Blind Veterans UK.

Hospital funding also came from commercial concerns. The Auctioneers and Estate Agents Institute raised funds to purchase the old Star & Garter Hotel on Richmond Hill and passed the deeds to Queen Mary, who had requested the British Red Cross Society to find a permanent home for the severely disabled young men returning from the battlefields. The Star & Garter Home welcomed its first residents in January 1916 but the premises were only intended as a temporary solution. The home's open ward is pictured opposite. The former hotel was subsequently demolished and a new home opened on the site in October 1924.

Netley and Chailey

The need for vast new hospital facilities at the start of the Great War sparked a rush to requisition, purloin and adapt any suitable buildings available. Existing hospitals were moved to new sites to free up their buildings for treatment of the military, as in the case of the Bethnal Green Infirmary in East London, which became the Bethnal Green Military Hospital under London District Command with 709 beds. The newly built HM Stationery Office warehouse building on Stamford Street, close to Waterloo Station, was transformed into the King George Military Hospital in 1915 and was for a while the largest such hospital in Britain with 1,900 beds. Convoys of the wounded were taken from Waterloo into the hospital via tunnels, to keep them out of public view. Again, huge charitable donations boosted the facilities, including £4,000 from the British Farmers' Red Cross Fund which was used to equip the operating theatres and the X-ray department.

For a while, the patient capacity of the King George Military Hospital eclipsed even that of easily the most famous military hospital in the country, at Netley in Hampshire. Built close to Southampton docks and opened in 1863, the Royal Victoria Hospital at Netley (pictured below, from the air) was the largest

purpose-built military hospital in the world and also the home of the Army Medical School. Popularly known as 'the palace of pain', the huge complex was extended during the Great War to include a Red Cross hospital and a separate Welsh Hospital funded by the people of Wales and under the command of Lieut. Col. H.G. Cook RAMC. In total, Netley had around 2,500 beds and had treated over 50,000 patients by the end of the war.

Of all the hospitals that offered some measure of needlework therapy, Netley was the most high profile as the work of its Handicrafts Committee among wounded servicemen was featured in two major national newspapers, 'The Daily Sketch' and 'The Times'. Published in November 1916, 'The Daily Sketch' article was headlined 'Crippled Soldiers as Skilled Embroiderers' and included photographs of the men showing their work, which was displayed at an exhibition which 'half Hampshire went to see ... in the handicrafts room behind the towering central building of that great house of pain.' The items at the exhibition were then sold at the home of one Mrs Cazalet at Grosvenor Square in London's West End to raise funds for Netley's handicraft projects, with Princess Helena opening the proceedings.

The article described how the hospital's embroidery frame 'is not a mere tool of leisure, but a distraction from pain ... devices were wrought by the rough hands of fighting men - often maimed hands at that ... needlework and other crafts are not mere amusement for the wounded but have a distinctive creative and mind healing effect.' A man who had lost his arm, the writer noted, 'had only three fingers on his remaining hand. He has to burn the ends of his silks with his cigarette, because he cannot use scissors.'

Perhaps the most innovative approach to rehabilitation through activity was adopted at Chailey in Sussex, in wards established alongside the Heritage Craft Schools, the handicrafts-based educational and medical institution for disabled children established by Grace Kimmins in 1903. As an article in the magazine 'Country Life' reported in 1916, the experiment in what was termed 'educative convalescence for the wounded' began when Colonel Edwin Hurry Fenwick, commander of the Bethnal Green Military Hospital, sent newly disabled servicemen to Chailey to recover with the personal assistance of the children themselves, who acted as their orderlies. The belief was that the men would retrain their motor skills and adapt better to amputation or paraplegia with the children as guides and examples.

An inveterate fund raiser and publicist for what became nationally known as 'the Heritage', Grace Kimmins oversaw the expansion of its military wards into the Princess Louise Special Military Hospital with £5,000 from another of Victoria's daughters, Princess Louise herself. In time, wounded servicemen came to Chailey from other hospitals in Sussex, Kent and London, including the men listed on pages 53 and 55. These particular pages do not name the hospital, but the identical illustration on each features an emblem that appears to blend a needle, crutch and sword. The chairman and founder of Chailey's medical board, the orthopaedic surgeon Sir Robert Jones, put together a photographic album now in the possession of East Sussex County Council. In a caption to a photograph of the embroidery class, he specifically mentions the contribution that its members - 'from Africa, Canada, New Zealand as well as the home country' - made to the St Paul's altar frontal.

From all corners of the Empire

Hospitals were also established for troops of specific nationalities. Over half of all doctors registered in Canada went overseas to serve in the Canadian Army Medical Corps (CAMC) and worked either in front line hospitals or at British-based but CAMC-run hospitals such as the Ontario Military Hospital in Orpington. The latter was opened in October 1914 and included a handicrafts room where Queen Victoria's granddaughter, Princess Patricia of Connaught, taught needlework to patients. Other Canadian hospitals were based at Epsom, Folkestone, Wokingham, Hastings, Bromley, Taplow and elsewhere, but it was not unusual to find large numbers of injured Canadian troops in any military hospital, anywhere in Britain. Fourteen such men, all contributors to the altar frontal, were treated at Highfield Hall Red Cross Hospital in Southampton in the months following the end of the war.

The 470-bed No. 2 Australian Auxiliary Hospital in Southall was opened in August 1916 for the treatment of Australian troops, following the success of the No. 1 Australian Auxiliary Hospital established at Harefield, Middlesex. Managed by the Australian Medical Corps and boasting an operating theatre that was funded by the Colonial Bank of Australasia, it was sited in the buildings of St Marylebone School and specialised in the care of amputees and the fitting of artificial limbs. It was to Southall that many of those wounded so terribly on the beaches of Gallipoli came in 1915-16, following the disastrous British campaign to create a new war front in the Dardanelles. The hospital closed in April 1919, so the 35 Australians listed in the Memorial Book as contributors to the altar frontal are likely to have been among its last patients.

Also on the western outskirts of London, in Richmond Park, was the South African Military Hospital. Work started in March 1916 and was completed four months later, when it was taken over by the Deputy Director of Medical Services, London District, on behalf of the Army Council as a gift from the South African people. Funds for the hospital's expansion were provided by a German-born financier, Otto Beit, who had interests in the South African gold and diamond industry.

The frontal design

Turning to the altar frontal itself, the first page of the Memorial Book tells us that the right hand panel was worked by men from the Dominions of Canada, Australia, New Zealand and South Africa, while the left hand panel and the rest of the fabric was the work of servicemen from the United Kingdom. A report of the July 1919 thanksgiving service in 'The Times' states that the idea to place a chalice at the centre of the design came from a 19 year old rifleman who can only have been Private Walter Conway of the Irish Rifles. Beyond this, however, we have no record of precisely which men worked on which part of the frontal, nor of which hospitals were responsible for which sections.

The official name for an altar frontal is an 'antependium'. Although the use of a frontal has always been optional in Holy Communion, altar cloths were used as far back as the fourth century. Just as the altar cloths represent the shroud of Christ, so the frontal symbolises what Geoffrey Webb in his book 'The Liturgical Altar' calls 'a covering of honour for the body of the altar which ... represents Christ Himself.'

The altar frontal created for St Paul's follows the traditional Roman form of five panels divided vertically by narrow strips of braid. Symmetric in its design, it follows traditions and precedents going back many centuries while remaining very emblematic of its time in its use of religious symbols and flora and fauna. Most striking is the boldness of its colours, chosen not just to add a sense of splendour and grace but because the altar frontal would be required to be seen across some distance. Red symbolises the blood of Christ on Good Friday and the holy fire of Pentecost, while green usually symbolises hope and white represents purity.

The design itself bears a strong Arts and Crafts influence and is in many ways a classic example of late 19th century/early 20th century 'art needlework', whose aesthetic was based on encouraging self-expression and reviving techniques rooted in the Middle Ages. The design features intricate floral patterns alternating with two palm branches in golden silk, which signify resurrection - victory over death itself. In the central panel is the grail or chalice of the Eucharist, representing Christ's suffering for the forgiveness of sin, above floral sheaths. As the picture on page 8 shows, the cup is studded with red cabochons - red representing the blood of Christ - while the flowers themselves were clearly chosen for their symbolism. Daisies represent innocence and purity while the tulip is a traditional symbol of gratitude. We know from the family of Lance Corporal James Muth that at least one of the tulips on the frontal was his work.

The pink and white flowers with long stamens are either lilies or passion flowers, both of which have strong Christian associations - indeed, the name of the passion flower is derived from the passion of Christ and its radial filaments are held to represent the crown of thorns. Lilies are a traditional symbol of purity. The red and pink flowers at the bottom of each panel are carnations, representing a mother's undying love. The large blue flower with a yellow centre at the bottom middle of each panel is probably a cornflower, signifying rebirth.

The birds of the frontal appear to be a hoopoe (also known as a lapwing) and a parrot. The brightly coloured and crested hoopoe (pictured on page 8) is symbolic of filial piety and devotion; a common species in the Middle East, it was adopted as the national bird of Israel in 2008. The inclusion of a parrot (page 25) is intriguing, as it is a southern hemisphere bird best known in Britain as an exotic pet, but it may simply indicate that the work on this side of the design was completed by servicemen from Australian regiments. Nevertheless, parrots were featured regularly in art from the 17th century onwards, sometimes as a sign of status but occasionally associated with the gift of prophecy.

The frontal fabric is an example of an appliqué, a needlework technique in which a piece of cloth or other material is laid on top of another larger piece and the two are stitched together, often to create a decorative effect. The use of appliqué can be traced back at least 3,300 years and may be even older. The altar frontal is fashioned from a cream silk damask, which is decorated with appliqué pieces that are themselves embellished with couching, gold thread, embroidered pieces and gems of various kinds.

The design was realised using the traditional technique of 'prick and pounce' - a method of transferring an embroidery design by using a pattern pricked with tiny holes, placed on the fabric, and then pounced all over with a powder made from cuttlefish bone that filters into the tiny holes to leave tiny dots on the fabric.

The Memorial Book

In contrast to the altar frontal, which was a product of forethought, planning and mathematical precision, the Memorial Book is an engagingly haphazard work. It had no display purpose and each hospital was free to contribute a page just as the individual appointed to the task felt fit. In some cases, that individual was clearly an artist of some distinction, possibly even a local professional. Other pages are much more obviously the work of amateur artists, affectingly hand painted with comparatively primitive lettering.

The pages record the names of the men who worked on the frontal, in some cases with full regimental information and the name of the hospitals treating them. The original book is made up of individual leaves of paper or parchment, all bound together in teal coloured leather with gold tooling by the foremost contemporary master of the technique, Sir Edward Sullivan. Although the unifying themes are thanksgiving and remembrance, each page has been decorated very differently. The page from Bethnal Green Military Hospital, for example, is drawn very simply in pen and ink, and it includes an intricate representation of the hospital's facade. By contrast, the Durris Auxiliary Hospital page is strikingly elaborate in its depiction of interweaving branches, men in hospital blues, and four regimental badges.

There are some puzzles here. The Highfield Red Cross Hospital in Southampton runs to three pages and credits the design and illustrative work to a CQMS (Company Quartermaster Sergeant) of the Devon Regiment whose signature is unfortunately indecipherable. One page features proudly the New Zealand coat of arms, a serving soldier and a Maori warrior, with a cameo of a cemetery, but carries neither a single name nor that of any of the men treated there. Its completion was probably overtaken by events in the rush to demobilise.

Research and restoration

Restoration of any piece of embroidery is an art in itself and the results achieved by the St Paul's broderers ('broderer' being a medieval word for embroiderer) have been breathtaking. Beginning with the restretching of the fabric on an oak frame, the whole process of restoration took six months, with the volunteer team working on the altar frontal project two days a week. Before the actual repair work could begin, much time was spent on delicately clearing the frontal of dust using special vacuum cleaners. Some of the original semi-precious (carnelian) stone cabochons were missing or loose so replacements were sourced and sewn into place.

Alongside the restoration, the painstaking task began of finding out more about the contributors to the altar frontal. Sources included service records, pension cards and the rolls of servicemen who were issued the Silver War Badge on being discharged due to wounds or sickness. Other information was provided by regimental archives and organisations such as the Western Front Association (WFA).

Appeals for help on the St Paul's web site and via the media resulted in a fairly limited response and it was at this point that Jane Robinson took on the task of tracing the families, using family history web sites and other resources. It is thanks to her hard work that so many of the relatives were contacted. Some of the relatives were able to provide photographs, stories and even examples of needlework completed by the men after demobilisation, which were then featured on the St Paul's web pages. Many of the stories that emerged were heartening.

Lance Corporal Alfred Westley of the Australian Imperial Force, an amputee, eventually became the Assistant Manager of the Repatriation Department of the Artificial Limb Factory in Victoria and was awarded the Imperial Services Medal for his work in 1959. Another amputee, Private Eric Alexander from New South Wales, returned to farming and went on to found a prizewinning Merino sheep stud.

While many of the men lived to a grand old age, others were far less fortunate. Private Alfred Applin of the Dorset Regiment was wounded at Gallipoli and died in May 1920 after spending nearly four years at The Star & Garter Home in Richmond. Australian Private John Till suffered multiple gunshot wounds near Ypres, had his left leg amputated and was moved to Southall. He succumbed to influenza just days after his discharge and died on 22nd February 1919. Private Conrad Tindall was the son of the Australian artist Charles Tindall; after his left leg was amputated, he was brought home to New South Wales on the hospital ship 'Karoola' to be cared for by his parents until his death in 1948. His father's painting of the ship, entitled 'Returned from the War', is now in a public gallery in Sydney.

The St Paul's Broderers
The team of restorers comprised (under the guidance of Teresa Heady the Cathedral Conservator): Anita Ferrero, Athalie Colqhoun, Jean Brazier, Ruth Cousins, Margaret Gibberd, Judy Hardy, Lianne Hart, Margaret Heighton, Diana Howarth, Isobel Lattimore, Sophia Sladden, Daphne Plaice-Leary, Rachel Rice, Helen Williams.

The altar frontal pictured during restoration in the broderers' workroom at St Paul's Cathedral.

HRH The Duchess of Gloucester, in her role as Patron of the Friends of St Paul's Cathedral, takes a close look at the altar frontal during its restoration.

The legacy of conflict

Much has been written during the centenary commemorations about the legacy of the Great War. For those who served and survived, the years after were spent adjusting to the new reality of 'Civvy Street'. For those left with severe disabilities - there were 240,000 amputees among British forces alone - the problems were hugely magnified, especially when it came to long term care and employment. At a time when 58 per cent of all unemployed men were ex-servicemen, many had war-related disabilities and an unknown number suffered what we would now call prolonged post-traumatic stress. While pensions were provided in most cases, much of the responsibility for care fell on to the shoulders of close family. The sight of limbless ex-servicemen on the streets selling matches to scrape a living became a source of national shame.

The voluntary agencies established during the war did what they could to ease the plight of the demobbed and disabled in the post-war years. The Soldiers and Sailors Families Association, founded in 1885 and a huge source of support and comfort during the war years, became the Soldiers, Sailors and Airmen Families Association (SSAFA) in 1918 under the presidency of Queen Alexandra, while the Royal British Legion was founded in 1921 as a voice for the ex-service community. St Dunstan's carried on its rehabilitation work with veterans who had lost their sight in the war, initially at Regent's Park and from 1927 at premises in Brighton. Some organisations were even set up to provide employment in embroidery.

Lady Londonderry, formerly Edith Chaplin, was President of the Women's War Services Legion, which, as well as providing cooks and drivers to the Army, established a School of Embroidery in London's Oxford Street to teach sailors and soldiers to make gold embroidery for uniforms. A charity called the Friends of the Poor started the Soldier Embroidery Industry in 1918 at 42 Ebury Street, London, with practical support from the Royal School of Needlework. The men usually worked from home on church embroideries such as a huge altar piece for St George's Chapel at Windsor Castle, commissioned by Princess Mary herself.

One of the real medical legacies of the war was the development of occupational therapy, which built on some of the lessons learned in the military hospitals of England and came to be considered an essential part of the treatment for people with physical and psychiatric disorders. By the time of the Second World War, therapies and treatment protocols were much more formalised and widely approved, and shell shock was recognised as a distinct condition. That needlework continued to play an important role in rehabilitation is shown by the popularity of a booklet called 'Needlecraft for HM Forces by Penelope', which was supplied by William Briggs and Co. under licence from the Board of Trade and sold for a shilling to soldiers in military and civilian hospitals. Inside each envelope were traced fabric, a needle, material to finish and an instruction chart. As the packaging put it, the packets were 'designed to foster a love of beautiful things, and the satisfaction which arises from the practice of personal skill.'

Life after war
The story of the altar frontal does not end with its restoration and display at St Paul's, nor with this book. Research is always an ongoing process and can never be complete. Much remains undiscovered and untold and it is hoped that the publication of this volume will bring forth yet further information. Behind a lot of the names recorded in the Memorial Book are whole life stories that remain tantalisingly out of reach. What became of these men? How did their war experience shape their lives? More mundanely, was their brief exposure to the joys and rewards of embroidery the sum of their involvement with this most ancient of crafts?

We do know from the families who contacted St Paul's following the appeal for information that some did indeed keep up their embroidery after the war. Peter, the nephew of Private Jim Allen of the 27th Battalion, Australian Imperial Force, remembered his uncle embroidering the Rising Sun, the emblem of the Australian Army, when he returned home. Private John 'Jock' Cameron of the 31st Battalion, Australian Imperial Force, developed his embroidery, leatherwork and carpet making skills, all gained or enhanced during his rehabilitation at Southall.

One who turned his skill at handicrafts into a living was Private William Augustus Newark, who spent over a year at Netley after suffering gunshot wounds to his chest and abdomen during the Battle of Messines in June 1916. A needlepoint picture of a flower garden which he completed during his time at Netley is still in the family's possession.

All the frontal embroiderers are now long gone, of course, but they live on in the hearts and minds of relatives like Liz Housden, whose grandfather Private Charles Housden had his leg removed while serving in the 2nd Bedfordshires. As she wrote in a letter to St Paul's, '[He] was given a tin one. It had a lever at the knee, on the side, that he had to adjust when he wanted to sit down or stand up ... I had no appreciation of how difficult this made his life. I simply thought he was an exceptionally special grandfather because none of my friends had grandfathers with tin legs.'

Malcolm Muth, the son of Lance Corporal James Muth, offered a poignant summary of his father's post-war life in Canada that the Reverend Canon Michael Hampel quoted in his sermon at the rededication service for the altar frontal. 'My father often spoke of the kindness of the doctors, nurses, and others during his convalescence,' Malcolm wrote. 'He was wounded twice and gassed, and so spent a long time in hospitals in England and after he came home. He did more embroidery here. He died at age 83 after a useful life in the community: the father of seven children, carpenter, church elder, village councillor, and so much more.' Malcolm's son James not only bore his grandfather's name but entered the military himself, achieving the rank of Lieutenant Colonel in the Royal Canadian Regiment, and gave the reading at the service of rededication - a passage from the Prophecy of Micah (Micah 4: 3):

'They shall beat their swords into ploughshares, and their spears into pruning-hooks; nation shall not lift up sword against nation, neither shall they learn war any more; but they shall all sit under their own vines and under their own fig trees, and no one shall make them afraid.'

For those servicemen of many nations who returned from the Great War, the overwhelming hope was that they would be able - as the passage suggests - to renounce war forever and reclaim a life of peaceful, everyday endeavour. To do so was in its own way a triumph of life over death - a rising again - and to do anything less would have been a betrayal of the men left behind. While the altar frontal speaks volumes for the resilience, resolve and skill of the men who created it, it is to those comrades who did not return that it remains such a quiet, understated and unfailingly moving tribute.

THE
MEMORIAL BOOK

The striking cover design of the Memorial Book is the work of Sir Edward Sullivan, a master bookbinder renowned for his skill in gold tooling. A barrister and son of the former Chief Justice of Ireland, Sullivan published the first illustrated colour edition of the ancient Book of Kells in 1914.

At the centre of his design is the chalice, the simplicity of which contrasts with the intricacy and ornateness of the surrounding floral design and the rectangular border. The wording chosen for the cover, 'Pro aris et focis', was a motto adopted by numerous regiments in the United Kingdom and the Dominions, among them the Middlesex Yeomanry which had links with St Paul's. Its literal translation is 'for our altars and our hearths' but it is more commonly translated as 'for God and country'. Just below the words 'et focis' in tiny lettering is 'E.S. Aurifex'. This was Sullivan's pseudonym, 'aurifex' meaning a worker in gold.

---

*'For our altars and
our hearths'*

No record exists of the calligrapher who rendered the explanatory text on this opening page of the Memorial Book, but it is clearly the work of an experienced professional. The artistry of the lettering shows the influence of Edward Johnston, who in the years running up to the war had redefined British calligraphy through his writings, teaching and example. With their innocently executed motifs and sometimes uncertain word formation, most of the pages that follow offer a startling but poignant contrast to the precision demonstrated here.

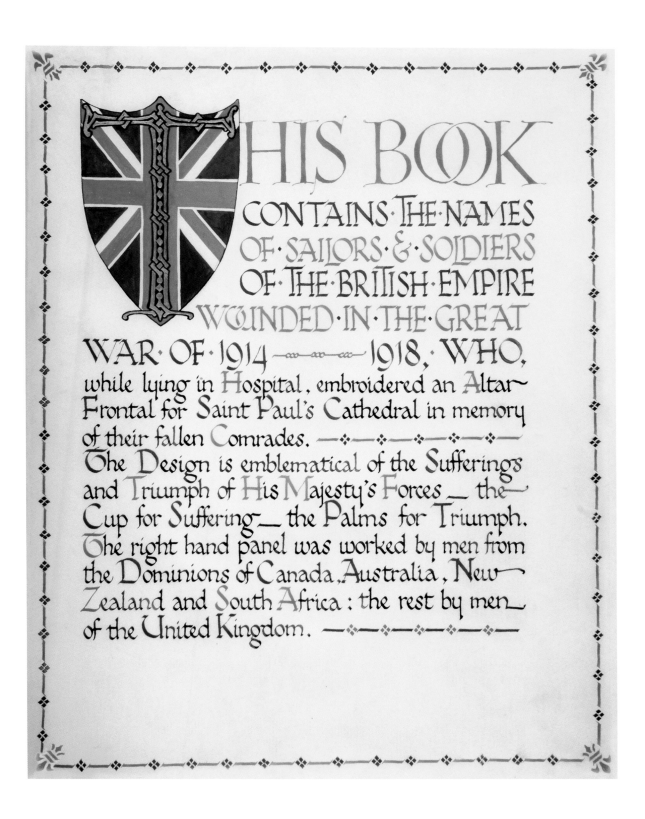

THIS BOOK CONTAINS·THE·NAMES OF·SAILORS·&·SOLDIERS OF·THE·BRITISH·EMPIRE WOUNDED·IN·THE·GREAT WAR·OF·1914 —∞—∞—∞— 1918, WHO, while lying in Hospital, embroidered an Altar Frontal for Saint Paul's Cathedral in memory of their fallen Comrades. —◆—◆—◆— The Design is emblematical of the Sufferings and Triumph of His Majesty's Forces — the Cup for Suffering — the Palms for Triumph. The right hand panel was worked by men from the Dominions of Canada, Australia, New Zealand and South Africa : the rest by men of the United Kingdom. —◆—◆—◆—

Just two names are recorded here below a representation of the chalice and a quotation from John 18:11. The hospital where **Rifleman Herbert Arthur Jenkins** and **Private Arthur Edward Scowen** were treated is not known, but the latter's service record shows that he lived in Paddington and was in the Territorial Force - the volunteer reserve component of the Army. He served from October 1914 to August 1918, when he was given a medical discharge due to unspecified wounds.

'The cup that my father has given me,
shall I not drink it?'

These are the words spoken by Jesus to the apostle Peter in the Garden of Gethsemane when he tries to prevent His arrest by the Temple guards. Knowing that death will follow, Jesus affirms that His sacrifice will fulfil the Scriptures in following the will of God. In this way Jesus gives the supreme example of readiness to lay down one's life for one's friends.

The Cup which My Father hath given Me shall I not drink it?

Rfm. Herbert Arthur Jenkins.
11th Battalion Rifle Brigade.

Pte. Arthur Edward Scowen

2nd Battalion. London Regt

Established by the Red Cross, The Star & Garter Home for Disabled Sailors, Soldiers and Airmen opened in the premises of a former hotel in Richmond in January 1916. Residents such as those listed opposite and pictured below were under the ultimate care of the Medical Superintendent, Major J. E. Dickie RAMC. The Home's committee included Sir Frederick Treves, Surgeon General to the King.

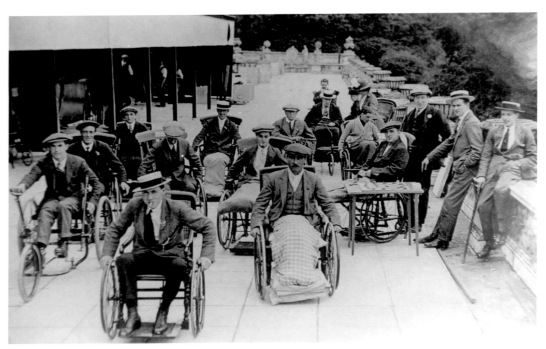

Private Richard Sibley of the Essex Regiment enlisted in January 1914 as a Special Reservist and was gassed at the second Battle of Ypres in May 1915. After recovering he returned to action and was severely wounded at Montauban in July 1916 during the Battle of the Somme. He was invalided from the Army in June 1917 and received a Silver War Badge in May 1919. He was transferred from Southwark Military Hospital to The Star & Garter Home in February 1919. In late 1921, as the document (right) shows, he was given a grant of £50 by the Military Service (Civil Liabilities) Department to start a shoe repair business. **Petty Officer Albert James Gutteridge** of the Royal Navy Air Service, whose name is listed on the next page, was given precisely the same grant for the same purpose just months later.

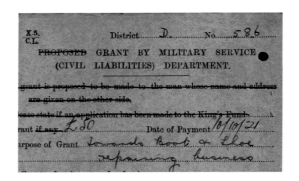

STAR & GARTER
RICHMOND

No 12646
Pte Alfred Applin
Machine Gunner
Dorset Regt

No 2153
Pte Richard Thomas Sibley
Machine Gunner
The Essex Regt

No. 19305.
Pte Samuel Cook.
5.th Royal Wiltshire Regt.

The servicemen listed here and on the following page were all cared for at The Star & Garter Home for Disabled Sailors, Soldiers and Airmen in Richmond. The three men named opposite were grouped together because of their naval service.

All three served in the Dardanelles. **Petty Officer Albert James Gutteridge** served with the Royal Naval Air Service as a mechanic and was shot in the spine at Gallipoli in September 1915, after which he was hospitalised in Malta and at Haslar Royal Navy Hospital in Gosport. He is pictured below right, in the cameo portrait and in hospital with his embroidery.

Private Frank Cox of the Royal Marine Light Infantry was shot in the back and chest at Gallipoli in the same month. He went on to wed Elsie Wright, the nurse who had cared for him. An illustration in an Italian newspaper (reproduced below) shows them being feted by well-wishers at their wedding in July 1925, after which they lived at Sir Oswald Stoll Mansions in Chelsea. Stoll was a theatrical impresario who set up his own Foundation to fund homes for servicemen injured in the Great War. For information on **Private William Charles Mesley**, see next page.

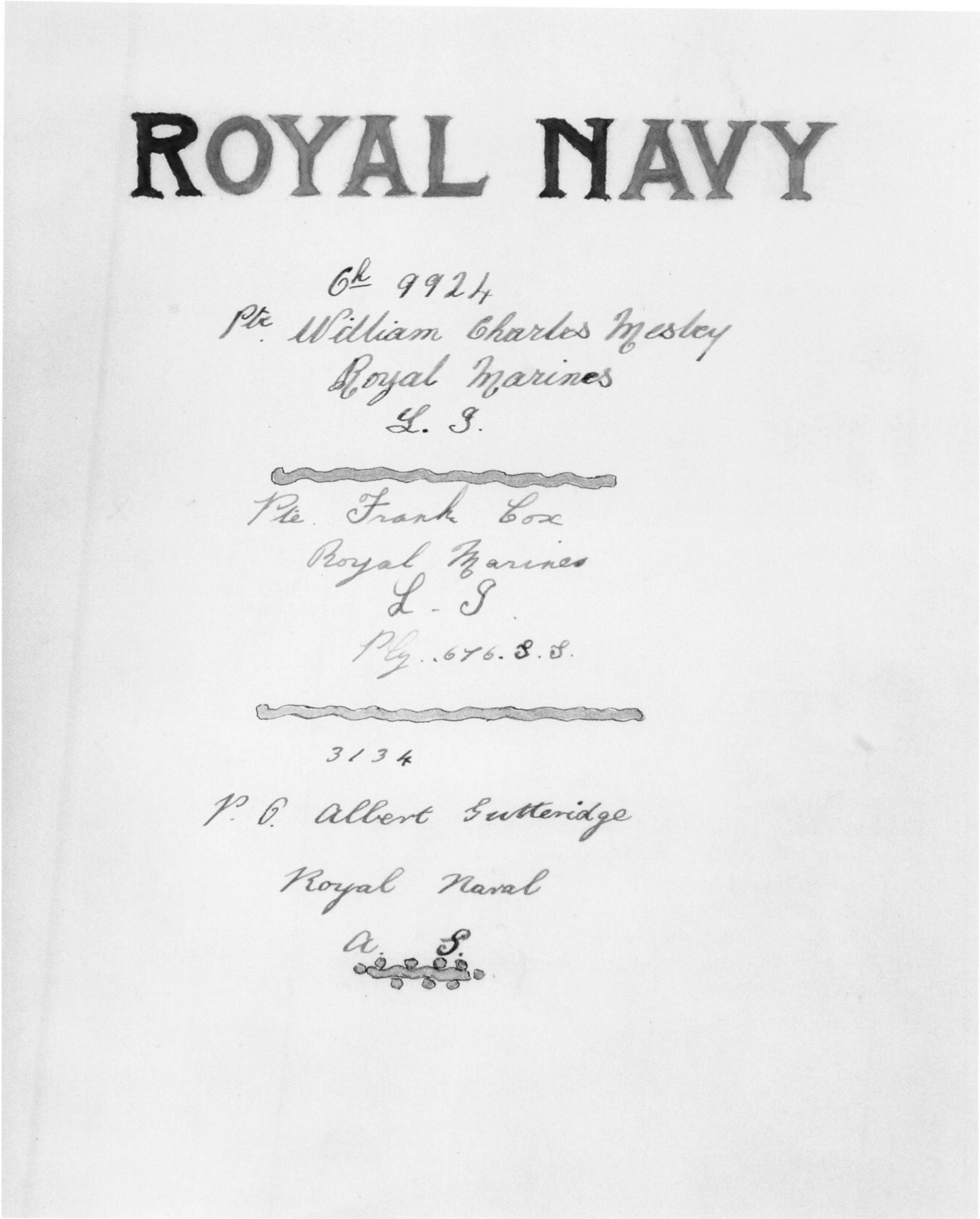

ROYAL NAVY

Ch 9924
Pte William Charles Mesley
Royal Marines
L. I.

Pte. Frank Cox
Royal Marines
L. I.
Plg. 676. S. S.

3134
P.O. Albert Gutteridge

Royal Naval

A. S.

Originally from Twickenham, **Private William Charles Mesley** joined the Royal Marines on his 16th birthday in 1894, served until 1905 and re-enlisted on the outbreak of war in 1914. One of the original British Expeditionary Force - the 'Old Contemptibles' - he was left paralysed in 1916 and later lost one of his legs. He is pictured above in his basket chair outside one of the huts at Netley, where he was treated prior to entering The Star & Garter Home.

Like his fellow Marine **Private Frank Cox** (see previous page), William was able to move to Sir Oswald Stoll Mansions, close to Chelsea Football Club where he watched matches regularly. On one occasion - captured on the front page of 'The Daily Graphic' in 1920 - he was introduced to the King. His granddaughter Joan Breacker recalls visiting him at home and watching him move the needle back and forth on a large embroidery frame.

No 11229
Pte John Robinson
East Yorkshire
Regt

_____

160920
Sgt R.F. Mundy.
10th Bn: Canadians

_____

4964
Pte J.W. Rickards
20th London
Regt

_____

2003
Pte. C. A. Rolfe.
3rd London Regt

Built on the personal instruction of Queen Victoria, the Royal Victoria Hospital at Netley was the largest purpose-built military hospital in the world when it opened its doors in 1863. It expanded massively during the Great War and had its own gasworks, bakery, reservoir and even a jail. Over 50,000 patients from all branches of the armed services had been treated there by the end of hostilities.

Private Albert Gilbert Macdermott (below left) was not yet 19 when his leg was amputated at Netley in February 1919, almost exactly one year after his enlistment in the Hampshire Regiment. He was discharged in March 1919.

Private William Augustus Newark (below right) was 34 years old when he enlisted in the 20th London Regiment in December 1915. He was hit by enemy fire during the Battle of Messines in June 1916 and was found after several days barely alive with gunshot wounds to his chest and abdomen. He would spend over a year at Netley.

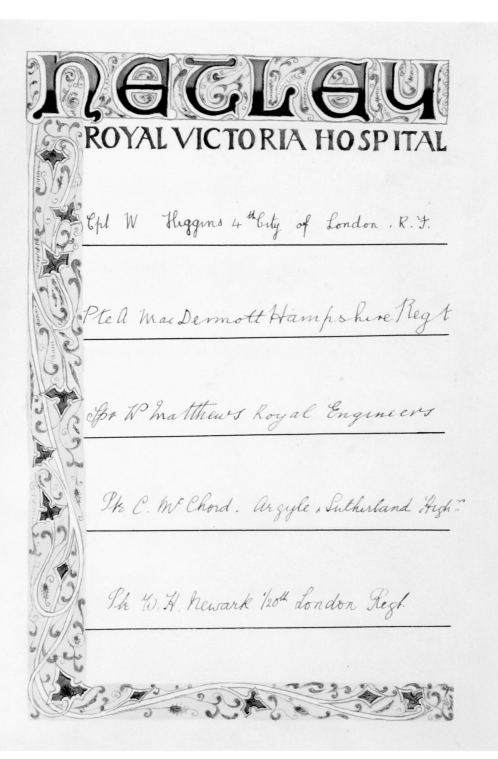

NETLEY
ROYAL VICTORIA HOSPITAL

Cpl W Higgins 4th City of London . R.F.

Pte A MacDermott Hampshire Regt

Spr W Matthews Royal Engineers

Pte C. McChord. Argyle & Sutherland High"

Pte W.H. Newark 1/20th London Regt.

The last name on this second page of Netley-based contributors is that of **Private William Glassby** of the York and Lancaster Regiment. He came from Barnsley and was discharged in July 1920, a full year after the altar frontal was dedicated. His recuperation following gunshot wounds was clearly a long one. As his pension record card (reproduced here) shows, he was awarded £1 a week in recognition of being 50 per cent disabled as a result of his war service.

'Wounded and shipwrecked' patients pose with nursing staff for a photograph in one of Netley's many wards.

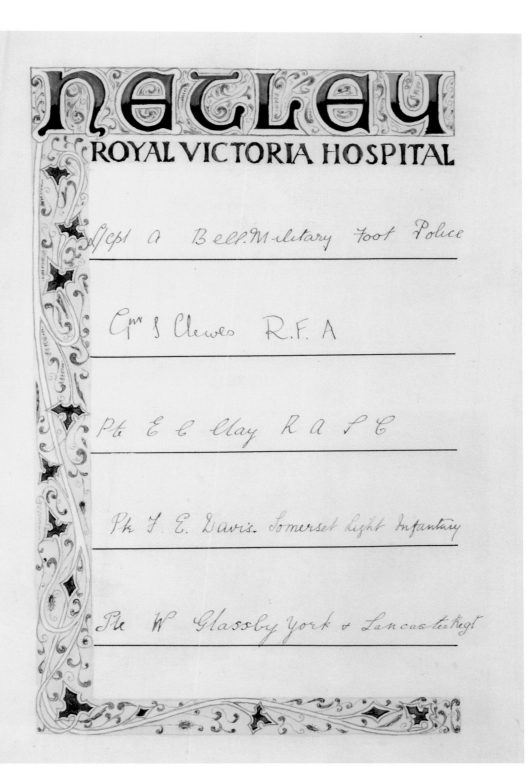

NETLEY

ROYAL VICTORIA HOSPITAL

L/Cpl A Bell. Military Foot Police

Gnr S Clewes R.F.A

Pte E C Clay R A S C

Pte F. E. Davis. Somerset Light Infantry

Pte W Glassby York & Lancaster Regt

As the spread of regiments in the list opposite demonstrates, Netley took patients from all branches of the forces. **Private Harold George Sadler** left his family in Bedford to emigrate to Canada and become a farmer. He enlisted in the Canadian Overseas Expeditionary Force in June 1915 at the age of 18 and served in the 20th Battalion, the Canadians. Wounded in France, he spent time at Netley where he painted and sketched and became one of the St Paul's altar frontal embroiderers. After returning to Canada, he moved to Buffalo, USA.

All manner of war-related injuries and conditions were treated in the vast facilities at Netley. The use of electrical therapy to treat neurasthenia, limb paralysis and what came to be termed shell shock was common. The Red Cross Hospital behind the main complex had a dedicated electrical treatment room, pictured here, that was made possible by donations from the philanthropist and Guinness company founder Viscount Iveagh and from the Maharaja of Gwalior, in appreciation of its treatment of Indian soldiers in 1914.

The electrical room at Netley. The placidity of the scene belies the well meant but often brutal nature of its treatment.

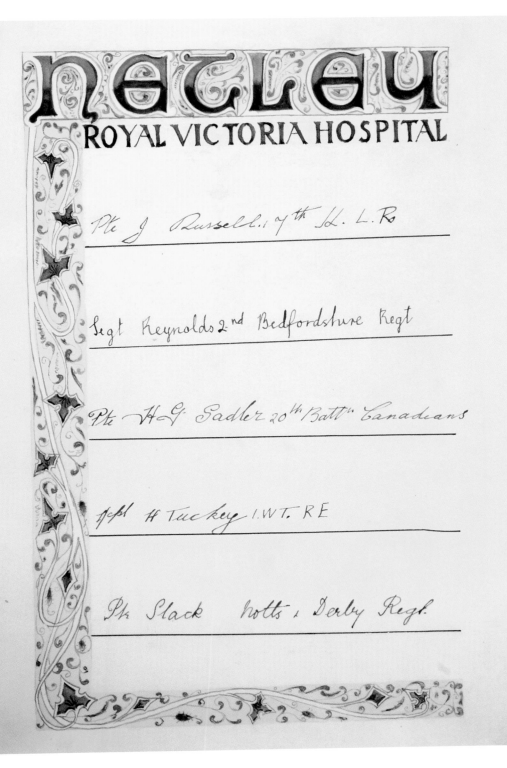

netley
ROYAL VICTORIA HOSPITAL

Pte J Russell. 17th H.L.R.

Segt Reynolds 2nd Bedfordshire Regt

Pte H.G. Sadler 20th Battn Canadians

Scpl H Tuckey I.WT. RE

Pte Slack   Notts & Derby Regt.

Netley was a huge complex incorporating the Royal Victoria Hospital and several specialist wings. The 500 bed Red Cross Hospital in the grounds (pictured below) was a 'hutted hospital' made up of 25 prefabricated temporary fieldhouses, each of which accommodated 25 patients. In his history of Netley, 'Spike Island: The Memory of a Military Hospital', Philip Hoare notes that 'beds were sponsored by local organisations and individuals, their contributions to the war effort marked by thick brass plates above the metal framed beds'.

Corporal John Levi Rose was born in Sturminster Newton, Dorset, and joined the 4th (Territorial Army) Battalion, the Dorsetshire Regiment, in 1912. He served in India, Egypt and Palestine and received a Territorial Forces War Medal, the least common of Great War Campaign Medals. **Private Herbert James Tilsed** of the

Machine Gun Corps was another native of Dorset (from Poole) and was treated in one of Netley's smaller hospitals, the Welsh Hospital. As his pension record (below) award document shows, Herbert's degree of disablement was re-assessed from 50 per cent to 30 per cent in the space of six months in 1920, reducing his weekly pension from a pound to 12 shillings.

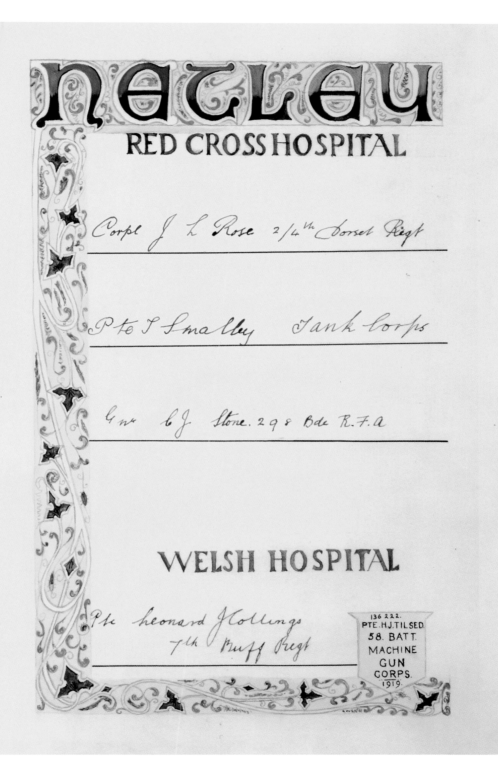

NETLEY

RED CROSS HOSPITAL

Corpl J L Rose 2/4th Dorset Regt

Pte S Smalley   Tank Corps

Gnr C J Stone. 298 Bde R.F.A

WELSH HOSPITAL

Pte Leonard Hollings
7th Buff Regt

136 222.
PTE. H.J. TILSED.
58. BATT.
MACHINE
GUN
CORPS.
1919.

As its name implies, the King George Military Hospital was one of many such institutions to enjoy royal patronage. It was opened by the Red Cross in 1915 in the premises of the vacated HM Stationery Office warehouse building on Stamford Street, close to Waterloo Station. Each of the five floors extended over an acre and a half. The hospital closed in June 1919, having treated around 71,000 men.

There is a tiny date at the foot of this page - July 1919 - that suggests this must have been one of the last pages to be completed and submitted prior to the dedication service at St Paul's that month.

Of the five servicemen listed here, no ranks are given, one lacks even a regiment, and little information is available on the others. We know that **John Walter Marshall** of the Grenadier Guards came from the Tyneside area and was discharged just days before the end of the war in November 1918, and that **Oliver Samuel** was from Blackwood in Monmouthshire and served as a Private in the Royal Fusiliers.

The roof of the King George Military Hospital with views towards St Paul's Cathedral.

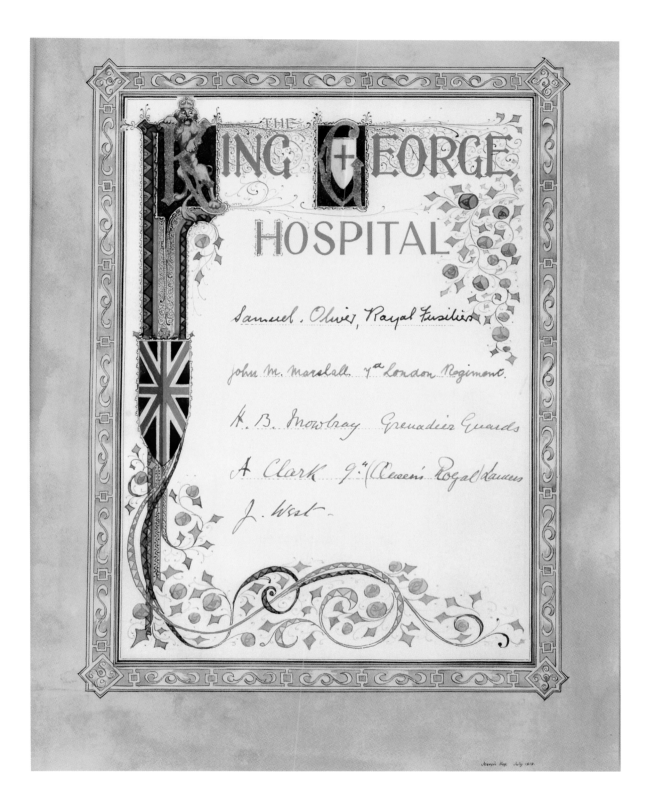

THE KING ✠ GEORGE HOSPITAL

Samuel. Oliver, Royal Fusiliers

John M. Marshall. 7ᵗʰ London Regiment.

H. B. Mowbray Grenadier Guards

A Clark 9ᵗʰ (Queen's Royal) Lancers

J. West.

St Dunstan's Lodge near Regent's Park became the headquarters of a charity for blinded servicemen set up by the future proprietor of 'The Daily Express', Arthur Pearson. As a hostel and training centre it welcomed over 1,300 blinded soldiers and sailors between 1915 and 1918.

One of the altar frontal embroiderers who spent time as a patient at St Dunstan's was **Quartermaster Sergeant George Eades**, who suffered a head injury and loss of sight in 1917. He was born in 1870, had served in the Boer War and had emigrated to Canada, where he managed a lumber company. He served in the Canadian Forestry Regiment during the Great War and arrived at St Dunstan's after his Army discharge in July 1918 where he became what the charity's records describe as a 'finished artiste' in embroidery.

The regard with which he was held is clear from the page opposite, which has a border depicting the mythical Gryphon - a creature whose feathers were said to cure blindness. He is also listed on the Highfield Hall Hospital page (see page 73), making him the only serviceman whose name appears twice in the record of those who embroidered the altar frontal.

George spent a short time in Canada as a teacher for the Canadian National Institute for the Blind (CNIB), before returning to his native Berkshire in 1922.

A huge number of illustrated postcards were sold in aid of St Dunstan's during the war years.

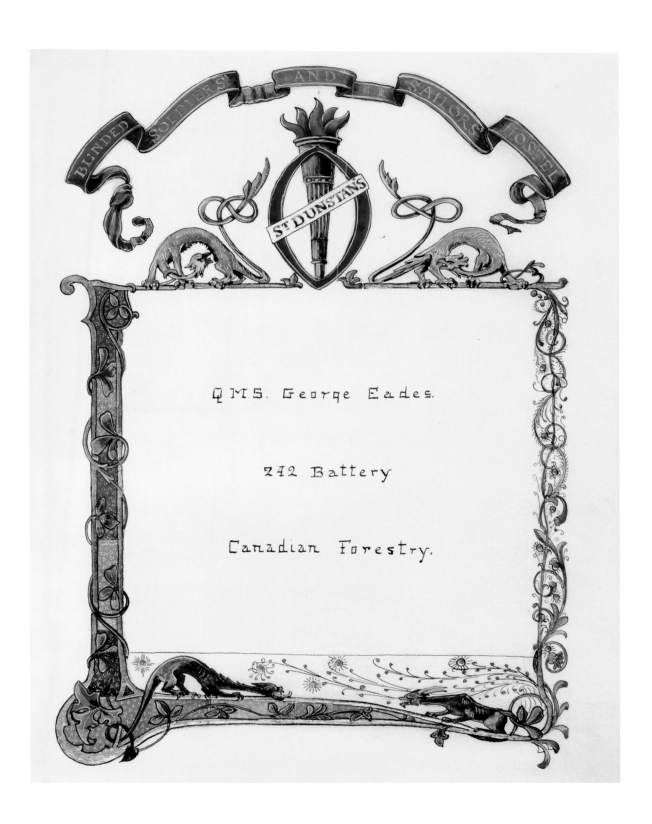

BLINDED SOLDIERS' AND SAILORS' HOSTEL

ST DUNSTANS

Q.M.S. George Eades.

242 Battery

Canadian Forestry.

The most finely illustrated of all the pages in the Memorial Book, this page was contributed by Durris Auxiliary Hospital in the town of Kirkton of Durris in Kincardineshire. The artist's name can be seen in the tiniest of script at the bottom centre of the page. The detail is stunning, from the multi-coloured foliage and the depiction of men in their blue hospital uniform to the badges on the right hand side, each of which represents the regiment of the adjacent named soldier.

The key name here is **Cadet Kenneth Alexander Baird** of the Inns of Court School of Law Officers Training Corps. He was wounded overseas and transferred to Durris from a hospital in Aberdeen. His parents owned the estate on which the hospital stood, which explains why his surname is so prominent and why their initials (HR & FK for Henry Robert and Florence Katherine) are incorporated into the design. 'The London Gazette' relates that Kenneth was later seconded to the Seaforth Highlanders as a temporary 2nd Lieutenant. After his marriage to Ernestine in 1924, he spent much of the rest of his life in Africa. We can only wonder whether one of the injured soldiers in the illustration on the left is Kenneth himself.

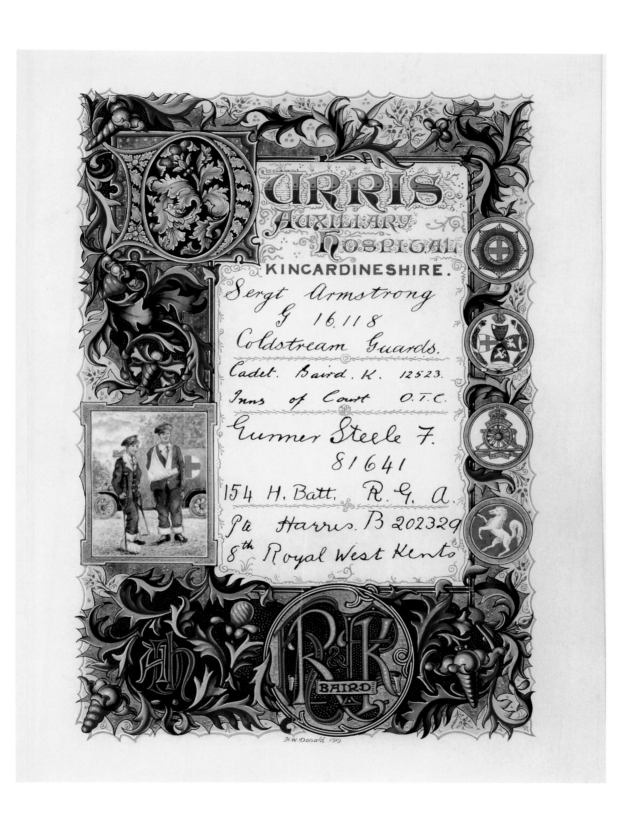

DURRIS
AUXILIARY
HOSPITAL
KINCARDINESHIRE.

Sergt Armstrong
G 16.118
Coldstream Guards.
Cadet. Baird. K. 12523.
Inns of Court O.T.C.
Gunner Steele F.
81641
154 H. Batt. R.G.A.
Pte Harris. B 202329
8th Royal West Kents

H.W.Donald 1919

For some time it was assumed that this and the following page were continuations of the Durris page, but the discovery that two of the men - **Private Augustus Cecil Wren** and **Private Wilfred Dexter** - spent a period of recovery at Chailey in East Sussex switched the focus to one of the most remarkable wartime hospitals of all. At the Princess Louise Special Military Hospital, principles of 'educative convalescence' were followed, where wounded servicemen were encouraged to adapt to their new disabilities with the assistance of disabled boys from Chailey Heritage School.

Private Augustus Cecil Wren of the Bedfordshire Regiment came from Lemsford in Hertfordshire and was treated in Edenbridge, Kent, before finding himself at Chailey for convalesence. Gus, as he was known, turned 20 years old on the first day of the war and enlisted soon after with his elder brother Frederick. Their younger brother Christopher - apparently named after the great architect of St Paul's - was killed on the third day of the Battle of the Somme, 3rd July 1916. After his return to Lemsford, Gus worked as a gardener at nearby Brocket Hall where Frederick was an under footman. He is pictured in both photographs below. In the right hand picture, he is the figure on the right standing next to an unidentified comrade.

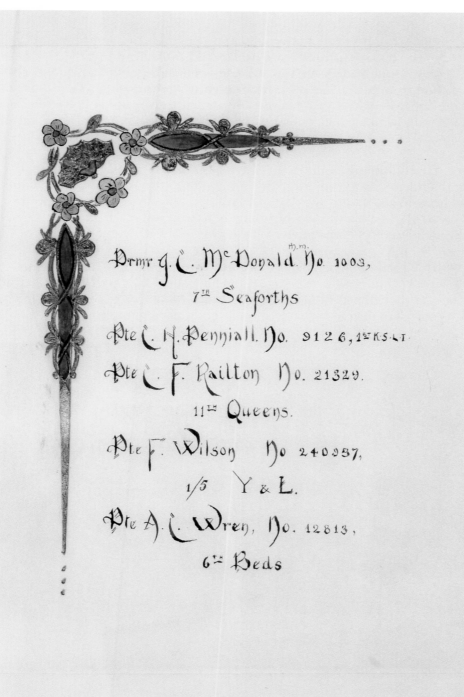

Drmr J. C. McDonald. No. 1003,
7TH Seaforths

Pte C. H. Penniall. No. 9126, 1st KSLI

Pte C. F. Railton No. 21329.
11th Queens.

Pte F. Wilson No. 240937,
1/5 Y & L.

Pte A. C. Wren, No. 12813,
6th Beds

Wounded soldiers would often find themselves back in Blighty but still a long way from home. **Gunner John McDonald** came from Inverness and served in the Seaforth Highlanders, **Private Charles Penniall** from Shropshire, **Private Fred Wilson** from South Yorkshire and **Sergeant Arthur Joines** from Jersey. Like Londoners **Private Cyril Frank Railton** and **Driver John Leitham**, they spent the months following the end of the war at Chailey and became members of the hospital's embroidery class that helped create the St Paul's altar frontal.

Private Alfred Morton of the Army Service Corps, Mechanical Transport, clearly did not let his war injuries stop him pursuing driving as an occupation. He was granted £50 by the Military Service (Civil Liabilities) Department in September 1919 as a deposit towards the purchase of a taxi cab, presumably to carry passengers around his home town of Guildford.

From North Witham in Lincolnshire, **Private Horace Wilfred Dexter** joined the Lincolnshire Regiment when he was 16 and later served in the Essex and Suffolk Regiments. Although he lost his left leg in action, he played in Chailey's stoolball team - a sport akin to cricket that is still played in parts of Sussex.

The embroidery class at Chailey. This photograph was included in an album made by Sir Robert Jones, chairman and founder of Chailey's medical board. The accompanying caption in the album notes that the class 'embroidered part of the Altar Frontal which was presented to St Paul's Cathedral'.

Spr H. A. Casey, No. 548819. R. E.

Pte. H. W. Dexter, No 42627,

12ᵗʰ Sflk. Regt.

Sgt A.A. Joines, No. 1446, ³/¹⁰ Ldn.

Dvr J. Leitham, No. 027097. A.S.C.

Pte A. Morton. No 264654,

A.S.C. M.T.

The Lady George Nevill Hospital was founded in Hove in 1917 by Lady George herself, next door to her home in Palmeira Drive. **Private Herbert Richard Barnes** of the 13th Battalion, Essex Regiment, kept a diary in which he recorded his wounding - on 13th November 1916 at 'about 5.30 in the morning' - during the very last days of the Battle of the Somme. He had an operation to remove pieces of shell three days later.

Back in Britain, Herbert was treated at a satellite hospital of the Lady George Nevill Hospital, Beechlands Hospital in Newick, very close to Chailey. After the war he used £35 granted to him by the Military Service (Civil Liabilities) Department to open a household goods shop in his home district of Leyton. As the photograph below shows, he proudly displayed his membership of the Essex Regiment on his store front.

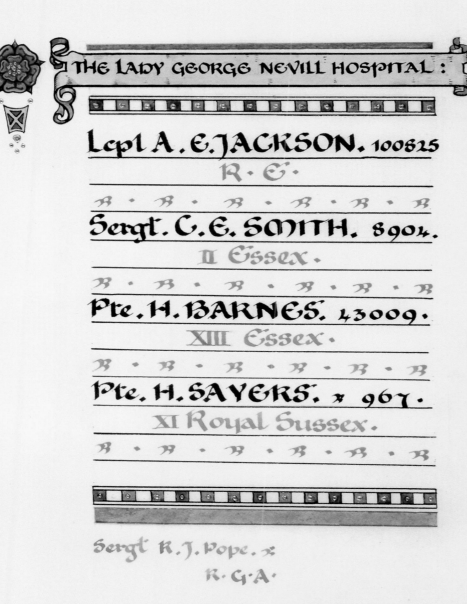

THE LADY GEORGE NEVILL HOSPITAL :

Lcpl A . E . JACKSON. 100825
R . E .

Sergt . C . E . SMITH . 8904 .
II Essex .

Pte . H . BARNES . 43009 .
XIII Essex .

Pte . H . SAYERS . x 967 .
XI Royal Sussex .

Sergt K . J . Pope . x
R . G . A .

Plans for a VAD Hospital in Bishop's Stortford were made as early as 8th August 1914 by Miss Fanny Stacey, who became Matron and oversaw its eventual move to Dane House, a mansion built in 1905 by the department store tycoon Sir John Barker of Barkers of Kensington fame. Only one name is included here - **Private Francis Purkiss** of the 8th Royal Dublin Fusiliers - but, judging by the space left for further signatures, there were probably more servicemen involved who were either discharged or transferred before they could add their own names.

County branches of the Red Cross created their own groups of volunteers called Voluntary Aid Detachments. Over 38,000 VAD members worked as assistant nurses, ambulance drivers and cooks during the Great War.

VAD Hospital, Bishops Stortford

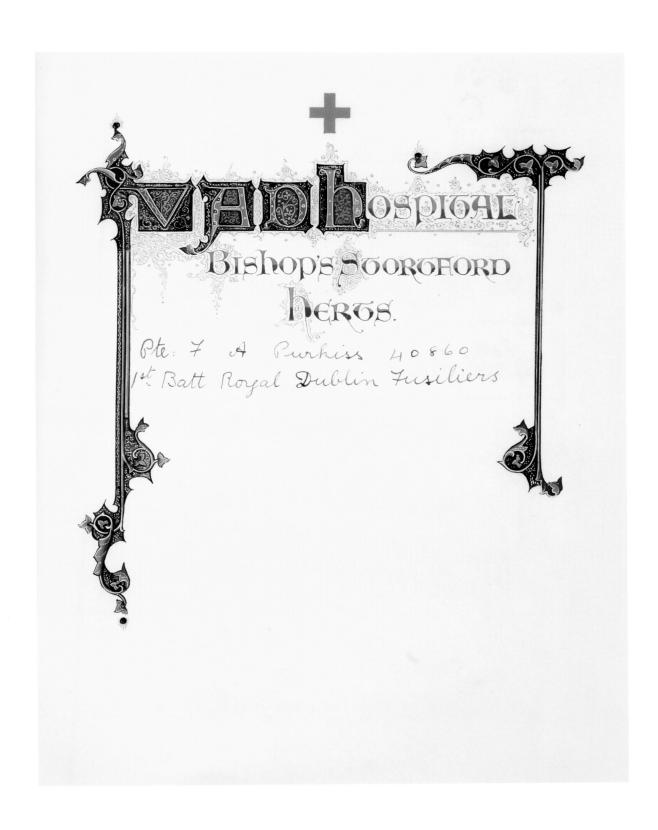

VAD Hospital
Bishop's Stortford
Herts.

Pte. 7 A Purkiss 40860
1st Batt Royal Dublin Fusiliers

Bethnal Green Hospital was opened in 1900 but was put to military use in 1915 under the command of the noted surgeon Colonel E. Hurry Fenwick. The illustration opposite shows the front entrance of the hospital as it looked in 1919. Events such as carnivals and bazaars helped raise funds, as the programme below shows.

Corporal Frederick Weedon of the 2nd Bedfordshire Regiment was wounded by a gunshot to the abdomen in April 1917 that meant a lengthy recovery and a spell at Bethnal Green. The reason for **Private Frederick Bird**'s hospitalisation cannot be traced but he enlisted in the Duke of Cornwall's Light Infantry months before the outbreak of war, in May 1914, and served on the Western Front and in Macedonia. Because conscription was not implemented in Ireland, losses to Irish regiments were made good by transferring soldiers from other regiments, so this may account for Frederick's subsequent transfer to the 2nd Battalion, Royal Dublin Fusiliers.

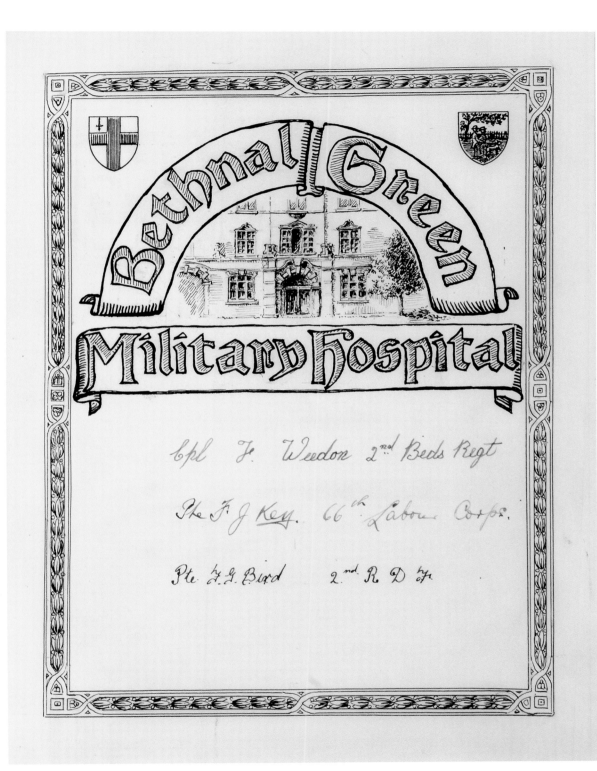

Cpl F. Weedon 2nd Beds Regt

Pte F. J. Key. 66th Labour Corps.

Pte F. G. Bird 2nd R D by

The Royal National Orthopaedic Hospital on London's Great Portland Street became a major centre for the treatment of newly disabled servicemen from late 1914 onwards. Its reputation for orthopaedic innovation grew rapidly and in 1920 the hospital moved to a new site on the edge of London at Stanmore, which it still occupies.

Rifleman Walter Conway, whose signature appears on the hospital's second page of names, was from Stepney and enlisted in the London Regiment in February 1914. He was later transferred to the Belfast-based 17th Battalion of the Royal Irish Rifles. He was almost certainly the man referred to in an article published in 'The Times' in July 1919 about the St Paul's altar frontal. According to the report, an unnamed 19-year-old rifleman had suggested that the chalice be the centre piece of the frontal. Walter was the only known 19-year old rifleman among the contributors.

'Rifleman Conway suggested that the chalice be the centre piece of the frontal'

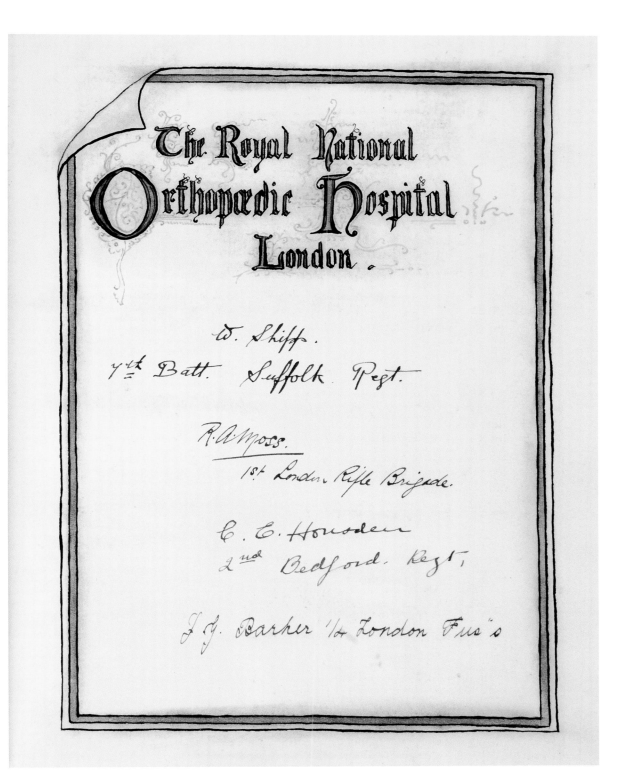

The Royal National
Orthopædic Hospital
London.

W. Shipp.
7th Batt. Suffolk Regt.

R. A. Moss.
1st London Rifle Brigade.

C. C. Housden
2nd Bedford. Regt,

J. J. Barker 1/4 London Fus's

Driver **Percy Cooney** (pictured below) was another veteran granted a post-war home in Sir Oswald Stoll Mansions. His story reached St Paul's via a letter from his daughter-in-law Jill, who explained that he was from the East End of London, attended the Duke of York Military School and worked as a ship steward and coal miner before joining the Royal Artillery in 1914. When his horse reared up after a shell exploded, Percy was trapped underneath and his stirrup pierced his ankle. When gangrene set in he had his left foot amputated.

It was at the Royal National Orthopaedic Hospital that he learned needlepoint. During a visit by Queen Alexandra, Percy was approached by an equerry who enquired if she could have his needlework of a bulldog straddling the world. Percy explained that he had promised it to his sister Mabel but that Her Majesty could have any of the other items. The Queen chose one and a few days later Percy received a tin of tobacco, £5 and a note of thanks.

Private Henry Maxwell of 1st Battalion, Wiltshire Regiment, was the only known Prisoner of War among the contributors to the altar frontal. He was initially reported as having been killed in action but in fact he was being treated in Germany for a severe leg fracture following his capture. He was sent to the Royal Orthopaedic Hospital after his arrival at Berne in neutral Switzerland in June 1918.

J. Hugo. 1st Batt. Devon Regt

S Sturgess #7 North Staffs

H.A. Maxwell. 1st Wiltshire Regt

Walter Conway   10th Royal Irish
                        Rifles.

George Kent - Pte 5th Northants.
Private Frederic John Young.
        11th Royal Fusiliers.

Driver. P. P. Cooney R. F. A.

In November 1914 the manufacturer and philanthropist Viscount Leverhulme - founder of Lever Brothers - offered his property in Hampstead, London, to the War Office for use as a hospital. Operating as **Cedar Lawn Auxiliary Military Hospital**, it was part funded by the Mayoress of Hampstead's Fund and treated a total of 2,383 patients before its closure in 1919. It then became a maternity home for the wives of servicemen financed by Queen Mary's Needlework Guild. Remarkably, the hospital recorded only two deaths during its existence.

Only two names appear on the page contributed by Cedar Lawn Hospital, both gunners in the Royal Field Artillery. The Celtic-style design - like a piece of ecclesiastical embroidery in itself - is not only strikingly different from that found on all of the other pages, it is also the most puzzling. Look closely and you will see serpent's heads, exotic birds and even (hidden in the letter 'h') a figure who may represent Christ.

Highfield Hall Red Cross Hospital used part of the buildings previously occupied by Southampton University College and was run by the college's principal, the highly regarded biologist Professor Alexander Hill.

Unusually, this page credits its artist, though deciphering the signature has not proved possible and we know only that he was a Company Quartermaster Sergeant in the Devon Regiment. The signature above his is that of Company **Sergeant Major Henry Brammer**, who enlisted in the King's Own Royal Lancaster in 1892 at the age of 14. He left the Army in 1910 with a Long Service and Good Conduct Medal but re-enlisted in December 1914. He transferred to the Essex Regiment in late 1917 and was wounded on 14th October 1918. After his discharge he lived in Carnforth, Lancashire, and died in 1944. 'The London Gazette' of 14th May 1919 records that he was awarded the Military Medal for bravery in the field.

Sgt Henry Brammer is pictured on the far right with his fellow winners of the Mounted Infantry Cup rifle competition in Malta, 1903.

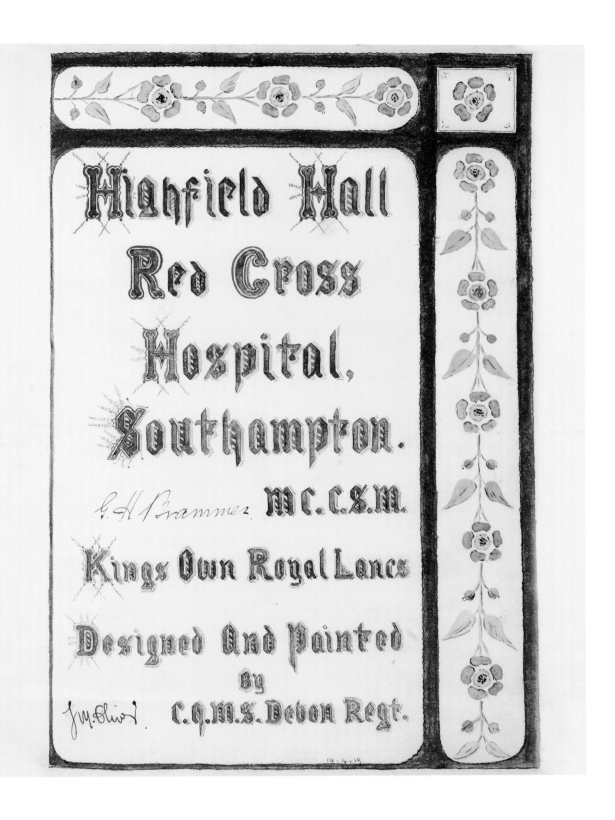

Highfield Hall
Red Cross
Hospital,
Southampton.
M.C.C.S.M.
G.H Brammer
Kings Own Royal Lancs
Designed And Painted
By
C.Q.M.S. Devon Regt.
J.M. Oliver.
19.4.19

Headed by a tableau graced with maple leaves, the next two pages of the Memorial Book remind us of the enormous contribution to the war effort made by the people of Canada in general and the men of the Canadian Expeditionary Force in particular. From a population of under eight million, Canada sent a force of 630,000 men, around 60,000 of whom lost their lives.

These were men who in most cases had left Britain in the early 1900s for a better life, never expecting that they would return just a few years later to take up arms against Germany. **Private Hedley George Brasnett** was a Norfolk man who settled in Saskatchewan; **Private William Oswald Hoodless** was originally from Lincolnshire and at the time of his attestation in 1916 was a clerk in Macleod, Alberta; **Private Edward Hodder** came from Loughborough and moved to Paris, Ontario, to work in the hosiery trade; **Staff Sgt Joseph Allan Lynas** was originally from Yorkshire and on his attestation form poignantly listed his next of kin as his mother, left behind in Leeds. Others were Canadian-born, the sons of first generation migrants, like **Private Harold Erskine Crosby**, a carpenter from Yarmouth, Nova Scotia, and **Private George Arthur Perry**, a farmer from Punnichy, Saskatchewan, who is pictured above.

Harold L. Gibson	Private	1033235	R. C. R.,
George. A. Perry	Private	268128	5th Bn
Hedley. G. Brasnett	Private	115930	31st Bn
James Henry	Private	503201	15th Bn
William O. Hoodless	Private	895007	50th Bn
Charles. W. Russell	Private	166226	18th Bn
Wm. Spencer	L/Cpl	445684	42nd Bn
A. G. Grant	Spr.	922215	C. E.,

Soon after St Paul's Cathedral put out a call for information about the altar frontal servicemen, an email was received from Anna Muth of Port Dover, Ontario, the granddaughter of **Lance Corporal James Ernest Muth** (pictured below next to his attestation paper). Anna wrote that her grandfather was wounded in his forearm, thighs, legs and foot, and was initially treated at Wharncliffe War Hospital in Sheffield.

James's son Malcolm Muth, a minister of the Presbyterian Church added that 'he worked a tulip in the piece for St Paul's, but when he heard that the altar was destroyed in the war he assumed that the frontal was lost as well.' Malcolm's son, also named James Muth, gave a reading at the re-dedication service at St. Paul's in August 2014.

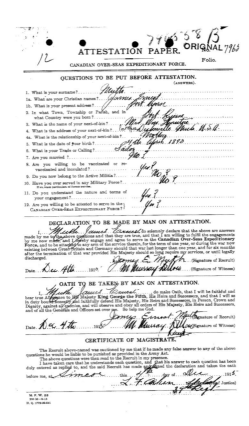

E. Hodder	Private	772149	87th Bn
J. Alden	Private	297663	78th Bn
S/Sgt. Lynas.	S/Sgt.	McG 236	P.P.C.L.I.
J. E. Muth	L/Cpl.	796558	7th C.E.
H. Crosby	Private	415858	24th Bn
Geo Eades	2.M.S	1048146	242nd Bn

The No. 2 Australian Auxiliary Hospital in Southall specialised in the care of amputees and was opened in August 1916 for the treatment of Australian troops. No fewer than 35 of its patients contributed to the St Paul's project - by far the largest number of contributors from any hospital.

A noted sprinter before the war, **Private Francis James Allen** of the 27th Battalion, Australian Imperial Force, lost a leg at Passchendaele and had the other amputated while recovering in England. The Allen family remember how he would propel himself on a board to get around after his return to Australia, and also that he rode a motorcycle and drove a car. He became very expert at sewing and embroidered the 'Rising Sun', the emblem of the Australian Army, when he got back to Australia, which the family still owns and is pictured here. The photograph of Jim below - he is third from the left at the front - was taken with fellow amputees while they were returning to Australia.

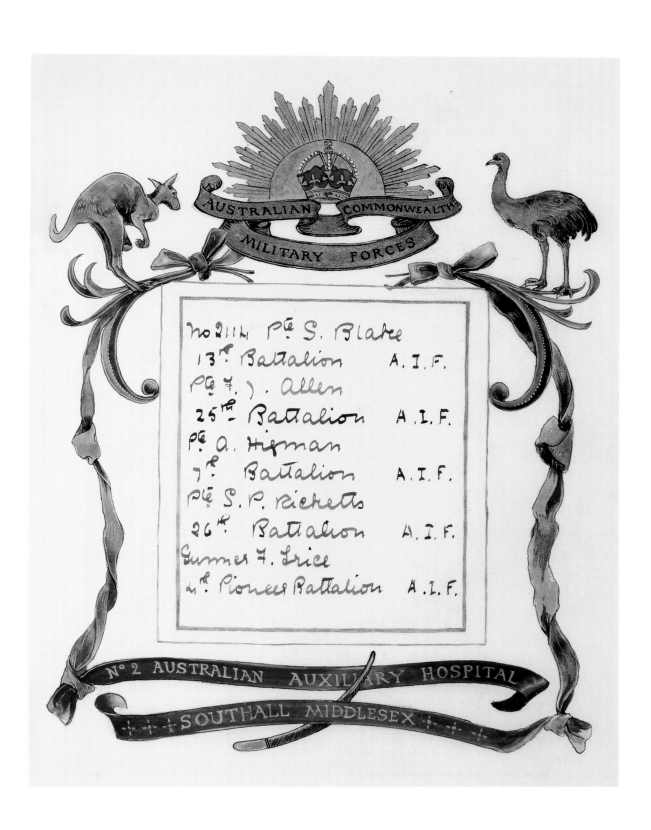

No 2114 Pte S. Blake
13th Battalion   A.I.F.
Pte F. J. Allen
25th Battalion   A.I.F.
Pte A. Hirman
7th Battalion   A.I.F.
Pte S. P. Ricketts
26th Battalion   A.I.F.
Gunner F. Price
4th Pioneer Battalion   A.I.F.

Nº 2 AUSTRALIAN AUXILIARY HOSPITAL
SOUTHALL MIDDLESEX

The patients at Southall who worked on the altar frontal included, unusually, four officers. **Private William Makeham** enlisted in July 1915 but was promoted to the rank of Lieutenant in less than three years. In April 1918 he was so badly wounded that his arm and leg had to be amputated.

Pictured below, **Captain Frederick Brooke Darling** of the Australian Field Artillery was a veteran of the ill-fated Gallipoli campaign and was awarded a Military Cross in 1916 'for conspicuous gallantry during a severe bombardment and enemy counter-attack.'

A bar was added to his Military Cross for his actions at Vortaverm on 10th April 1918 when, as the citation read, 'he, with three men, brought into action under exceptionally heavy fire a mortar belonging to another unit, and fired several rounds into the enemy when practically surrounded by them. He was severely wounded, two of his three men were killed, while the third managed to fight his way back to his battery.' His injuries necessitated the amputation of his right leg and a period of convalescence at Southall before his return to Australia in May 1919.

Capt F. B. Darling   8th Field Art

Capt P. H. Goldstein   55th Batt

Lieut J. W. Stubbs   8th Batt

Lieut N. W. Makeham   8th Machine Guns

Sergt W. Lynch   52nd Batt

Lance Corp C. Bickley   59th Batt

Lance Corp W. Williams   8th Batt

Pte W. Gillies   17th Batt

Pte W. Macarthy   2nd Pioneers

The list of Australian servicemen who worked on the altar frontal at Southall continues on to this third page, though the fact that all the names are written in one hand suggests that it may have been made up after the men had been shipped back. Among the names are **Private Eric George Alexander** from New South Wales and Tasmania-born **Sergeant Major Frederick Ripper**, who lost a leg and arm respectively in action in France.

The list also includes **Private George Ernest Doddridge** (left) from Angaston, South Australia, who served with the 10th Battalion, Australian Imperial Force, at Gallipoli, Alexandria and in northern France. He was wounded in July 1916, returned to action but was wounded again in May 1918. He arrived in England in June 1918 on the hospital ship SS Jan Breydel and was sent to a hospital in Birmingham, where his right leg was amputated above the knee. He was moved to Southall where he stayed until March 1919.

Private John Cameron (left) of the 31st Battalion originally came from Aberdeenshire and had a weak right eye but excellent vision in his left. The accuracy of his shooting enabled him to enlist, in spite of this disability. He was wounded on 1st October 1918 and had his left leg amputated below the knee at Graylingwell Hospital in Chichester. He was admitted to Southall in March 1919 and was discharged three months later.

The collar badge of John Cameron's regiment, the 31st Battalion, Kennedy Regiment, with its distinctive emblem of two intertwined boomerangs. The regiment was named after the Queensland explorer Edmund Kennedy.

No. 1611	Pte E. Alexander	56th	Battalion	A.I.F.
No. 1080	Pte H.J. Clarke	19th	"	A.I.F.
No. 3192	Pte J. Cameron	31st	"	A.I.F.
No. 938	Pte G.E. Doddridge	10th	"	A.I.F.
No. 31717	Gunner C.K. Gunn	54th	Battery	Aust Field Arty
No. 3385	Pte W. Gosper	54th	Battalion	A.I.F.
No. 2581	Sergt C. Hughes	56th	"	A.I.F.
No. 6083	Pte A. Kennedy	24th	"	A.I.F.
No. 2090	Sergt F.J. Kingsbury	34th	"	A.I.F.
No. 14034	Sapper C.H. Marchant	3rd	Engineers	A.I.F.
No. 8190	Pte M. O'Brien	1st	Battalion	A.I.F.
No. 6868	Pte W. Olsen	22nd	"	A.I.F.
No. 1677	Pte W.H. Smith	42nd	"	A.I.F.
	Pte J. Sill	54th	"	A.I.F.
No. 7093	Pte C.S. Lindall	4th	"	A.I.F.
No. 134	Pte C.S.M. Ripper	12th	"	A.I.F.
No. 210	Pte J.C. Swainston	44th	"	A.I.F.
No. 3618	Pte H. Van Viest	35th	"	A.I.F.
No. 2944	L. Corpl A.H. Westley	23rd	"	A.I.F.
No. 3674	Pte A.J. Nixon	49th	"	A.I.F.
No. 11183	Gunner J. Young	54th	Battery	A.F.A.

Just over 100,000 New Zealanders served in the First World War, over half of whom were casualties: 16,700 were killed and well over 40,000 wounded. One of the great unknowns of the altar frontal project is how many servicemen from New Zealand contributed to it while in hospital in Britain. Even the name of the hospital itself is not recorded, though hospitals serving the wounded of the New Zealand Expeditionary Force (NZEF) were established at Brockenhurst, Walton-on-Thames, Codford, Hornchurch and elsewhere.

With its depiction of a soldier in the uniform of the NZEF and a warrior in Maori costume, set against a landscape of river and mountains and headed by the New Zealand armorial bearings, the page opposite was clearly created with care and love in readiness for their signatures or at least their names. It is most likely that all had been taken aboard ships bound for home before this could be done.

'Over 100,000 New Zealanders served in the First World War'

New Zealand

South Africa had enjoyed Dominion status within the British Empire since 1910, but a residue of resentment remained among some white South Africans towards a country with which it had been at war just a few years before. South Africa's participation in the war on the British side nevertheless proved wholehearted and vital. Over 136,000 South African troops fought in the Middle East and on the Western Front; over 7,000 lost their lives and more than 12,000 were wounded.

Funded by the South African government, the South African Military Hospital was opened in 1916 on a 12 acre site in Richmond Park provided by King George V himself. It was paid for by the South African Hospital and Comforts Fund Committee, which comprised wealthy South Africans living in Britain.

Kimberley-born **Private Andrew Manzie** was living in Durban when he enlisted in the 2nd South African Infantry Regiment in 1917. He came to Richmond after losing his leg in action in France. **Private Henry Alfred Schroeder** from King William's Town served in the same battalion and was hospitalised at Richmond after sustaining a gunshot wound to the left thigh in October 1918. He was discharged on 29th April 1919. He is the seated soldier in the photograph below.

SOUTH AFRICAN MILITARY HOSPITAL
RICHMOND SURREY

9047. Lee/Cpl. Hampson. C.R. 2nd S.A.i.

13272 Pte. H.A. Schroeder 2nd S.A.i.

13533 Pte. A.J. Manzie 2nd S.A.I.

14891 Pte. E.A. Spurgeon S.A.M.C.

7967 Pte. W. Williams 2nd S.A.i.

14402 Sig. J.J. Germishuys. 1st S.A.I.

11553 Pte Dell. A.H. 3rd S.A.I.

13735 Pte Swart J.Z 1st S.A.I

The final page of the Memorial Book offers six further names of contributors, all patients at the South African Military Hospital in Richmond during the period between the Armistice in November 1918 and the Treaty of Versailles in July 1919 that formally ended the war.

The hospital was staffed by 13 officers of the South African Military Corps (SAMC). The presence in the list opposite of SAMC men **Lance Corporal William Alexander Thompson** - together with that of **Private Eric Spurgeon** on the preceding page - is a reminder of the bravery of the soldier-medics, who were responsible for the dangerous task of giving immediate treatment to the wounded and evacuating them from the battlefield.

 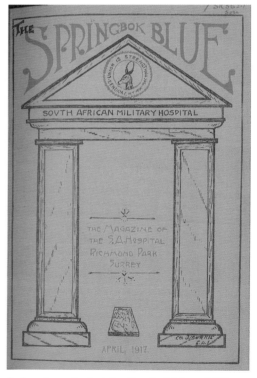

Dundee-born nurse Helen Bain (pictured above) worked at the South African Military Hospital from 1917 to 1919 and kept a photographic record which is now held in the archives of the London Borough of Richmond. The Springbok Blue was a magazine produced at the hospital for patients and staff.

10014 Pte L.S Dudley   2nd S. A. I.

5557. Sgt. E. H. Burns.   2nd S.A.I.

15934.   Norton Fred   4th S A Scotts.

12296 L/cpl. Thompson W.A. S.A.M.C

1638 Gnr. Turner W.H.A. S.A.H.A

9474 Pte Jansen F.A. 1st S A I

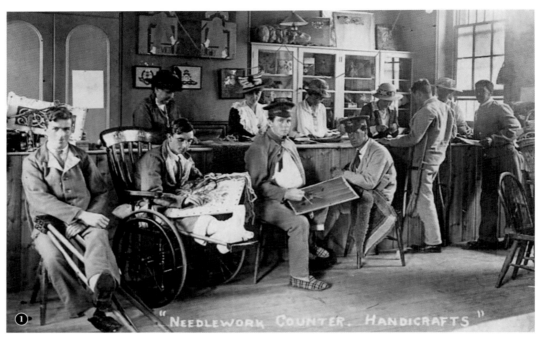

1. *Handicrafts at Netley - the needlework counter.* **2.** *Private Charles Edward Housden (standing, second from right), treated at the Royal National Orthopaedic Hospital in London.* **3.** *Private Arthur Jesse Winn, treated at the 2nd Australian Auxiliary Hospital at Southall.* **4.** *Private Eric George Alexander, treated at the 2nd Australian Auxiliary Hospital at Southall.* **5.** *Private Herbert James Clarke, treated at the 2nd Australian Auxiliary Hospital at Southall.*

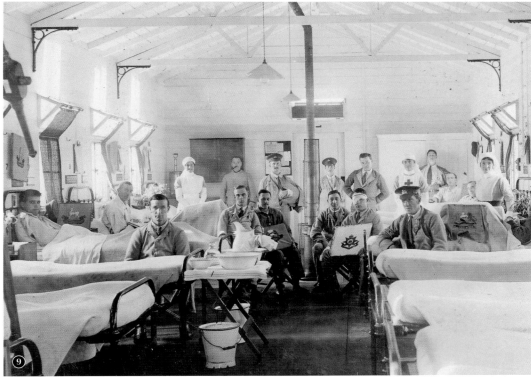

6. *Private Walter Smith, treated at the 2nd Australian Auxiliary Hospital in Southall.*
7. *Nurses and patients outside 'Derbyshire Hut No. 1', Netley.*
8. *Patients proudly display their embroidery at Netley.*
9. *With embroidery to hand, inside one of the Netley huts.*

Surname	First name	Rank	Service No.	Regiment	Name of Hospital	Regimental Nation
Jenkins	Herbert Arthur	Rifleman	N/A	11th Battalion Rifle Brigade	Unidentified Hospital	Great Britain
Scowen	Arthur Henry	PTE	N/A	2nd Battalion, London Regiment	Unidentified Hospital	Great Britain
Applin	Alfred	PTE	12646	5th Battalion, The 3rd Dorset Regiment	The Star and Garter Home, Richmond	Great Britain
Cook	Samuel Charles	PTE	19305	5th Royal Wiltshire Regiment	The Star and Garter Home, Richmond	Great Britain
Sibley	Richard Thomas	PTE	2153	Essex Regiment	The Star and Garter Home, Richmond	Great Britain
Cox	Frank	PTE	67688	Royal Marine Light Infantry	The Star and Garter Home, Richmond	Great Britain
Gutteridge	Albert James	PO (M)	F3134	Royal Navy Air Service	The Star and Garter Home, Richmond	Great Britain
Mesley	William Charles	PTE	9924	Royal Marine Light Infantry	The Star and Garter Home, Richmond	Great Britain
Mundy	Reginald Frank	SGT	160920	10th Battalion Canadians	The Star and Garter Home, Richmond	Canada
Richards	Joseph W.	PTE	4964	20th London Regiment	The Star and Garter Home, Richmond	Great Britain
Robinson	John	PTE	11229	East Yorkshire Regiment	The Star and Garter Home, Richmond	Great Britain
Rolfe	Cyril Abbott	PTE	2003	3rd London Regiment	The Star and Garter Home, Richmond	Great Britain
Higgins	W.	CPL	N/A	4th City of London Regiment	The Royal Victoria Hospital, Netley	Great Britain
MacDermot	Albert Gilbert	PTE	N/A	Hampshire Regiment	The Royal Victoria Hospital, Netley	Great Britain
Matthews	William Alfred	SPR	N/A	Royal Engineers	The Royal Victoria Hospital, Netley	Great Britain
McChord	Cormick W.	PTE	S/5892	Argyle and Sutherland Highlanders	The Royal Victoria Hospital, Netley	Great Britain
Newark	William Augustus	PTE	N/A	1/20th London Regiment	The Royal Victoria Hospital, Netley	Great Britain
Bell	Arthur John	L/CPL	P/10984	Military Foot Police	The Royal Victoria Hospital, Netley	Great Britain
Clay	Edward Lawrence	PTE	N/A	Royal Army Service Corps	The Royal Victoria Hospital, Netley	Canada
Cleeve	Samuel	Gunner	101658	Royal Field Artillery	The Royal Victoria Hospital, Netley	Great Britain
Davis	John Ernest	PTE	10725	Somerset Light Infantry	The Royal Victoria Hospital, Netley	Great Britain
Glassby	William	PTE	N/A	York and Lancaster Regiment	The Royal Victoria Hospital, Netley	Great Britain
Reynolds	Charles Howard	SGT	N/A	2nd Bedfordshire Regiment	The Royal Victoria Hospital, Netley	Great Britain
Russell	J.	PTE	N/A	17th King's Liverpool Regiment	The Royal Victoria Hospital, Netley	Great Britain
Sadler	Harold George	PTE	409183	20th Battalion Canadians	The Royal Victoria Hospital, Netley	Canada
Slack	N/A	PTE	N/A	Nottinghamshire & Derbyshire Regiment	The Royal Victoria Hospital, Netley	Great Britain
Tuckey	Thomas Henry	L/CPL	135615	Inland Water Transport, Royal Engineers	The Royal Victoria Hospital, Netley	Great Britain
Rose	John Levi	CPL	N/A	2/4th Dorset Regiment	Red Cross Hospital, Netley	Great Britain
Smalley	John	PTE	310467	Tanks Corps	Red Cross Hospital, Netley	Great Britain
Stone	C. J.	Gunner	N/A	298 Brigade, Royal Field Artillery	Red Cross Hospital, Netley	Great Britain
Collings	Leonard J.	PTE	N/A	7th Buffs Regiment (East Kent Regiment)	Welsh Hospital, Netley	Great Britain
Tilsed	Herbert James	PTE	136222	58 Battalion Machine Gun Corps	Welsh Hospital, Netley	Great Britain
Clark	A.	N/A	N/A	Queen's Royal Lancers	The King George Hospital, London	Great Britain
Marshall	John Walter	N/A	N/A	Grenadier Guards	The King George Hospital, London	Great Britain
Mowbray	Horace B.	N/A	N/A	Grenadier Guards	The King George Hospital, London	Great Britain
Samuel	Oliver	N/A	70459	Royal Fusiliers	The King George Hospital, London	Great Britain
West	J.	N/A	N/A	N/A	The King George Hospital, London	Great Britain
Eades	George	QMS	N/A	242 Battery Canadian Forestry	St Dunstan's, Blinded Soldiers and Sailors Hostel	Canada
Armstrong	George	SGT	16118	Coldstream Guards	Durris Auxiliary Hospital, Kincardineshire	Great Britain
Baird	Kenneth Alexander	CDT	12523	Inns of Court, Officer Training Corps	Durris Auxiliary Hospital, Kincardineshire	Great Britain
Harris	Bertrand Pearce	PTE	202329	8th Royal West Kents	Durris Auxiliary Hospital, Kincardineshire	Great Britain
Steel	Frederick	Gunner	81641	154th Battalion, Royal Garrison Artillery	Durris Auxiliary Hospital, Kincardineshire	Great Britain
McDonald	John Cameron	DRMR	1003	7th Seaforths	Chailey Hospital	Great Britain
Penniall	Charles H.	PTE	9126	1st King's Shropshire Light Infantry	Chailey Hospital	Great Britain
Railton	Cyril Frank	PTE	21329	11th Queen's	Chailey Hospital	Great Britain
Wilson	Fred	PTE	240937	1/5th York and Lancaster	Chailey Hospital	Great Britain
Wren	Augustus Cecil	PTE	12813	6th Bedfordshire	Chailey Hospital	Great Britain
Casey	Henry Alfred	SPR	548819	Royal Engineers	Chailey Hospital	Great Britain
Dexter	Horace Wilfred	PTE	42627	12th Suffolk Regiment	Chailey Hospital	Great Britain
Joines	Arthur A.	SGT	1446	1/19th London Regiment	Chailey Hospital	Great Britain
Leitham	John	DVR	27097	Army Service Corps	Chailey Hospital	Great Britain
Morton	Alfred	PTE	264654	Army Service Corps, Mechanical Transport	Chailey Hospital	Great Britain
Barnes	Herbert Richard	PTE	43009	13th Essex Regiment	The Lady George Nevill Hospital	Great Britain
Jackson	Alfred E.	L/CPL	100825	Royal Engineers	The Lady George Nevill Hospital	Great Britain
Pope	R.J.	SGT	N/A	Royal Garrison Artillery	The Lady George Nevill Hospital	Great Britain
Sayers	Herbert	PTE	5D/967	11th Royal Sussex Regiment	The Lady George Nevill Hospital	Great Britain
Smith	C. E.	SGT	8904	2nd Battalion, Essex Regiment	The Lady George Nevill Hospital	Great Britain
Purkiss	Francis A	PTE	40860	1st Battalion Royal Dublin Fusiliers	Voluntary Aid Detachment Hospital, Bishops Stortford	Ireland
Bird	Frederick G.	PTE	N/A	2nd Royal Dublin Fusiliers	Bethnal Green Military Hospital	Ireland
Key	F.J.	PTE	N/A	66th Labour Corps	Bethnal Green Military Hospital	Great Britain
Weedon	Frederick	CPL	13364	2nd Bedfordshire Regiment	Bethnal Green Military Hospital	Great Britain
Barker	J. G.	N/A	N/A	1/4th London Fusiliers	The Royal National Orthopaedic Hospital London	Great Britain
Housden	C. E.	N/A	N/A	2nd Bedfordshire Regiment	The Royal National Orthopaedic Hospital	Great Britain
Moss	R.A.	N/A	N/A	1st London Rifle Brigade	The Royal National Orthopaedic Hospital London	Great Britain
Shipp	William	N/A	N/A	7th Battalion Suffolk Regiment	The Royal National Orthopaedic Hospital	Great Britain
Conway	Walter	N/A	44630	10th Royal Irish Rifles	The Royal National Orthopaedic Hospital	Great Britain
Cooney	Percy Patrick	DVR	22737	Royal Field Artillery	The Royal National Orthopaedic Hospital	Great Britain
Hugo	John James Victor	N/A	N/A	1st Battalion, Devon Regiment	The Royal National Orthopaedic Hospital	Great Britain
Kent	George Arthur	PTE	N/A	5th Northamptonshire	The Royal National Orthopaedic Hospital	Great Britain

Surname	First name	Rank	Service No.	Regiment	Name of Hospital	Regimental Nation
Maxwell	Henry Alfred	N/A	10187	1st Wiltshire Regiment	The Royal National Orthopaedic Hospital	Great Britain
Sturgess	Samuel	PTE	12836	7th North Staffordshire Regiment	The Royal National Orthopaedic Hospital	Great Britain
Young	Frederic John	PTE	N/A	11th Royal Fusiliers	The Royal National Orthopaedic Hospital	Great Britain
Dench	William Charles	GNR	179040	Royal Field Artillery D Battery 75th Brigade	Cedar Lawn Auxilary Military Hospital	Great Britain
Wallace	Harold	GNR	172693	Regiment Canadian Artillery	Cedar Lawn Auxilary Military Hospital	Canada
Brammer	George Henry	N/A	16245	King's Own Royal Lancaster	Highfield Hall Red Cross Hospital, Southampton	Great Britain
Brasnett	Hedley George	PTE	115930	31st Battalion	Highfield Hall Red Cross Hospital, Southampton	Canada
Gibson	Harold Lawrence	PTE	1033235	Royal Canadian Regiment	Highfield Hall Red Cross Hospital, Southampton	Canada
Grant	Alexander Grewan	SPR	922215	Canadian Engineers	Highfield Hall Red Cross Hospital, Southampton	Canada
Henry	James	PTE	503201	15th Battalion	Highfield Hall Red Cross Hospital, Southampton	Great Britain
Hoodless	William Oswald	PTE	895001	50th Battalion	Highfield Hall Red Cross Hospital, Southampton	Canada
Perry	George Arthur	PTE	268128	5th Battalion	Highfield Hall Red Cross Hospital, Southampton	Canada
Russell	Charles William	PTE	166226	18th Battalion	Highfield Hall Red Cross Hospital, Southampton	Great Britain
Spencer	William	L/CPL	445684	42nd Battalion	Highfield Hall Red Cross Hospital, Southampton	Great Britain
Crosby	Harold Erskine	PTE	415858	24th Battalion	Highfield Hall Red Cross Hospital, Southampton	Canada
Eades	George	QMS	1048146	242nd Battalion	Highfield Hall Red Cross Hospital, Southampton	Canada
Hodder	Edward	PVT	772149	87th Battalion	Highfield Hall Red Cross Hospital, Southampton	Canada
Lynas	Joseph Allan	S/SGT	MCG236	Princess Patricia's Canadian Light Infantry	Highfield Hall Red Cross Hospital, Southampton	Canada
Muth	James Ernest	L/CPL	796558	133 Battalion, Royal Regiment of Canada	Highfield Hall Red Cross Hospital, Southampton	Canada
Olden	J.	PVT	297663	78th Battalion	Highfield Hall Red Cross Hospital, Southampton	Canada
Allen	Francis James	PTE	N/A	27th Battalion Australian Imperial Force	No. 2 Australian Auxiliary Hospital, Southall, Middlesex	Australia
Blake	Sidney	PTE	2114	13th Battalion Australian Imperial Force	No. 2 Australian Auxiliary Hospital, Southall, Middlesex	Australia
Higman	Albert	PTE	5093	7th Battalion Australian Imperial Force	No. 2 Australian Auxiliary Hospital, Southall, Middlesex	Australia
Ricketts	Sydney Talbot	PTE	3960	26th Battalion Australian Imperial Force	No. 2 Australian Auxiliary Hospital, Southall, Middlesex	Australia
Trice	Frederick	GNR	N/A	4th Pioneers Battalion Australian Imperial Force	No. 2 Australian Auxiliary Hospital, Southall, Middlesex	Australia
Bickley	Cecil	L/CPL	N/A	59th Battalion	No. 2 Australian Auxiliary Hospital, Southall, Middlesex	Australia
Darling	Frederick Brooke	CPT	4432	8th Field Artillery	No. 2 Australian Auxiliary Hospital, Southall, Middlesex	Australia
Gillies	William James Todd	PTE	6310	17th Battalion	No. 2 Australian Auxiliary Hospital, Southall, Middlesex	Australia
Goldstein	Percy Hirsch	CPT	N/A	55th Battalion	No. 2 Australian Auxiliary Hospital, Southall, Middlesex	Australia
Lynch	W. Clarence	SGT	N/A	52nd Battalion	No. 2 Australian Auxiliary Hospital, Southall, Middlesex	Australia
Macarthy	William	PTE	N/A	2nd Pioneers	No. 2 Australian Auxiliary Hospital, Southall, Middlesex	Australia
Makeham	William	LT	N/A	8th Machine Guns	No. 2 Australian Auxiliary Hospital, Southall, Middlesex	Australia
Stubbs	James Westralia	LT	N/A	8th Battalion	No. 2 Australian Auxiliary Hospital, Southall, Middlesex	Australia
Williams	W.	L/CPL	N/A	8th Battalion	No. 2 Australian Auxiliary Hospital, Southall, Middlesex	Australia
Alexander	Eric George	PTE	1611	56th Battalion Australian Imperial Force	No. 2 Australian Auxiliary Hospital, Southall, Middlesex	Australia
Cameron	John	PTE	3192	31st Battalion Australian Imperial Force	No. 2 Australian Auxiliary Hospital, Southall, Middlesex	Australia
Clarke	Herbert James	PTE	1080	19th Battalion Australian Imperial Force	No. 2 Australian Auxiliary Hospital, Southall, Middlesex	Australia
Doddridge	George Ernest	PTE	938	10th Battalion Australian Imperial Force	No. 2 Australian Auxiliary Hospital, Southall, Middlesex	Australia
Gosper	William	PTE	3385	54th Battalion Australian Imperial Force	No. 2 Australian Auxiliary Hospital, Southall, Middlesex	Australia
Gunn	Charles Kenneth	GNR	31717	54th Battalion Australian Imperial Force	No. 2 Australian Auxiliary Hospital, Southall, Middlesex	Australia
Hughes	Cecil	SGT	2581	56th Battalion Australian Imperial Force	No. 2 Australian Auxiliary Hospital, Southall, Middlesex	Australia
Kennedy	Arthur McLuer	PTE	6083	24th Battalion Australian Imperial Force	No. 2 Australian Auxiliary Hospital, Southall, Middlesex	Australia
Kingsbury	Frederick John	SGT	2090	34th Battalion Australian Imperial Force	No. 2 Australian Auxiliary Hospital, Southall, Middlesex	Australia
Marchant	Charles Henry	SPR	14034	3rd Engineers Australian Imperial Force	No. 2 Australian Auxiliary Hospital, Southall, Middlesex	Australia
O'Brien	Malcolm	PTE	8190	1st Battalion Australian Imperial Force	No. 2 Australian Auxiliary Hospital, Southall, Middlesex	Australia
Olsen	William Charles	PTE	6868	22nd Battalion Australian Imperial Force	No. 2 Australian Auxiliary Hospital, Southall, Middlesex	Australia
Ripper	C. S. M. Frederick Horace	PTE	134	12th Battalion Australian Imperial Force	No. 2 Australian Auxiliary Hospital, Southall, Middlesex	Australia
Smith	Walter Herbert	PTE	1677	42nd Australian Imperial Force	No. 2 Australian Auxiliary Hospital, Southall, Middlesex	Australia
Swainston	Tom Clyde	PTE	210	44th Battalion	No. 2 Australian Auxiliary Hospital, Southall, Middlesex	Australia
Till	John	PTE	5458	54th Battalion Australian Imperial Force	No. 2 Australian Auxiliary Hospital, Southall, Middlesex	Australia
Tindall	Conrad Lindsay	PTE	7093	4th Battalion Australian Imperial Force	No. 2 Australian Auxiliary Hospital, Southall, Middlesex	Australia
Van Diest	Hendrikus	PTE	3618	35th Battalion Australian Imperial Force	No. 2 Australian Auxiliary Hospital, Southall, Middlesex	Australia
Westley	Alfred Henry	L/CPL	2944	23rd Battalion Australian Imperial Force	No. 2 Australian Auxiliary Hospital, Southall, Middlesex	Australia
Winn	Arthur Jesse	PTE	3674	49th Battalion Australian Imperial Force	No. 2 Australian Auxiliary Hospital, Southall, Middlesex	Australia
Young	John	GNR	11183	54th Battery, Australian Field Artillery	No. 2 Australian Auxiliary Hospital, Southall, Middlesex	Australia
Dell	Arthur Henry	PTE	11553	3rd South African Infantry	South African Military Hospital, Richmond, Surrey	South Africa
Germishuys	Frans Jacobus	SIG	14402	1st South African Infantry	South African Military Hospital, Richmond, Surrey	South Africa
Hampson	C.R.	LT/CPL	9047	2nd South African Infantry	South African Military Hospital, Richmond, Surrey	South Africa
Manzie	Andrew John	PTE	13533	2nd South African Infantry	South African Military Hospital, Richmond, Surrey	South Africa
Schroeder	Henry Alfred	PTE	13272	2nd South African Infantry	South African Military Hospital, Richmond, Surrey	South Africa
Spurgeon	Eric A.	PTE	14891	South African Medical Corps	South African Military Hospital, Richmond, Surrey	South Africa
Swart	J. F.	PTE	13735	1st South African Infantry	South African Military Hospital, Richmond, Surrey	South Africa
Williams	W.	PTE	7967	2nd South African Infantry	South African Military Hospital, Richmond, Surrey	South Africa
Dudley	Lionel Stanley	PTE	10014	2nd South African Infantry	South African Military Hospital, Richmond, Surrey	South Africa
Dunne	E.H.	SGT	5557	2nd South African Infantry	South African Military Hospital, Richmond, Surrey	South Africa
Jansen	Frederick John	PTE	9444	1st South African Infantry	South African Military Hospital, Richmond, Surrey	South Africa
Thompson	William Alexander	L/CPL	12296	South African Medical Corps	South African Military Hospital, Richmond, Surrey	South Africa
Turner	W. Harold A.	GEN	1638	South African Heavy Artillery	South African Military Hospital, Richmond, Surrey	South Africa
Turton	S	N/A	15934	4th South African Scottish	South African Military Hospital, Richmond, Surrey	South Africa